Ghosts of Lincoln Park

A Chicago Hauntings Companion

Ursula Bielski

AMERICAN GHOST BOOKS

Copyright © 2024 by Ursula Bielski

American Ghost Books, an imprint of Sentia Publishing Company, has the exclusive rights to reproduce this work, to prepare derivative works from this work, to publicly distribute this work, to publicly perform this work, and to publicly display this work.

All rights reserved. No part of this publication may be reproduced, stored in a retrieval system, or transmitted, in any form or by any means, electronic, mechanical, photocopying, recording, or otherwise, without the prior written permission of the copyright owner.

Cover Illustrations by Anna Huffman
Printed in the United States of America
ISBN: 979-8-9915482-4-3

AUTHOR'S PREFACE:
AN UNCANNY ENCLAVE

As one of the oldest neighborhoods in Chicago, Lincoln Park is also, surely, one of the most haunted in the city. The home of Al Capone's arch-enemy, George "Bugs" Moran, Lincoln Park saw some of the worst Gangland violence in American history, including the 1929 St. Valentine's Day Massacre. Occurring in a narrow brick garage at 2122 North Clark Street, the slaughter was part of a Chicago almost as blighted as today's city by turf wars, shootings and death.

Lincoln Park also hosted one of the terrifying deaths which became known as the "Tylenol Murders." On October 1, 1982, flight attendant and Old Town resident Paula Prince was found dead two days after buying a bottle of the cyanide-laced capsules at the Walgreens store at North Avenue and Wells Street, in Lincoln Park's Old Town section.

Next door to the Second City comedy theater on Wells street was the infamously haunted Old Town restaurant called That Steak Joynt, an old-school eatery with one of the meanest ghosts in town, known to drag waitresses down the staircase and manifest as a pair of glowing eyes. Psychics and mediums claimed that a double murder had occurred in Piper's Alley, the cobblestoned pathway which once ran along the building, and that the killer, in phantom form, was still at large on the premises. The current restaurateur denies any ghostly goings-on today.

As we'll see, these and other dark doings played out on a truly ghostly stage: Chicago's original City Cemetery grounds that sprawled over a great expanse of this lakefront region of town.

I've been chasing Chicago's ghosts for nearly forty years, and we've been sharing them on Chicago Hauntings Tours for more than half that time. The tales in this book, then, were lovingly collected over decades, as I scoured both library microfilm and fading memories for the gems that we all treasure so much: the ghost stories of Chicago. I hope you enjoy this look at the true ghostlore of Lincoln Park: one of the city's most storied—and spirited—neighborhoods.

Happy Hauntings!
Ursula Bielski

CONTENTS

AUTHOR'S PREFACE: AN UNCANNY ENCLAVE	iii
HIDDEN TRUTHS	1
WILD NIGHTS	7
THE VAMPIRE HUNTERS	17
THE SUDDEN STORM	23
THE LAKE MICHIGAN TRIANGLE	29
TIES TO THE DEVIL	41
THE THUNDER-MAKER	55
THE BRIDGE OF SIGHS	59
"...OR WHATEVER IT WAS"	75
THE NIGHT CHICAGO DIED	79
SWEET HOME CHICAGO	89
THE MAGIC HEDGE	97
THE SPELL OF CRICKET HILL	101
CURTAINS FOR A DIRTY RAT	105
THE WOOD WALKERS	117
THE PRESIDENT, POST-MORTEM	121
AUTHOR'S AFTERWORD	125
ABOUT THE AUTHOR	127

HIDDEN TRUTHS

1

It seems that nearly every Chicagoan, and many a tourist for that matter, is aware that native businessman Ira Couch (1806--1857) is dead, though almost no one knows exactly who he was, what he did, or why his tomb stands in the middle of Lincoln Park. For generations, drivers along the park's rich sweep of green have ogled the hotelkeeper and realtor's somber tomb with a mixture of keen curiosity and frank unease, wondering at the explanation for this odd ornament affixed in the backyard of the Chicago History Museum.

Unknown to many natives and most tourists is the fact that the public playground that is today's Lincoln Park was once the civic cemetery. This aptly named Chicago City Cemetery stretched from present day Armitage Avenue south to the then city limits at (North Avenue), providing plots to the departed prairie-dwellers of earliest Chicago. Most of these were later

---

[1] Couch Tomb *Library of Congress*

disinterred and relocated to various sites around the city upon the closing of City Cemetery around 1870. When this mass evacuation began, the Couch family reportedly rallied and appealed to officials to let the tomb remain due to the cost of transporting the mausoleum to another site. In time, the city consented, and so the Couch tomb remains, though many historians believe that Ira Couch is actually interred in Rosehill Cemetery, along with the rest of the clan.

Before the establishment of City Cemetery, Chicago had made some poor decisions concerning the question of burial. The area's first homesteaders along the river had buried their kin in their backyards, leading to a few surprises later on when the downtown area was dug up to lay the foundations for skyscrapers and other developments. In addition, the Chicago River sometimes played tricks on the bereaved who might bid farewell to their loved ones only to watch them floating by on the waterway some time later, having been purged from their graves after a particularly heavy rain. Further, the two cemeteries that were finally established in 1835—a Protestant one at Chicago and Michigan avenues and a Catholic one near 23rd Street and Calumet Avenue—were both situated squarely on the lake shore, leading to the frequent unearthing of caskets. When population increases added to the inadequacy of the funerary system, the city selected acreage at Clark Street and North Avenue on which to found Chicago City Cemetery. Simultaneously, the Roman Catholic Diocese of Chicago secured for its faithful a portion of property between Dearborn and State streets, south of North Avenue. Though none of this land was exactly towering above the water table, any of it was preferable to the shaky sepulchers of the earliest burial grounds. The transfer of bodies to the new sites began at once.

Scarcely a decade after the opening of the new cemeteries, however, Chicagoans began to loudly complain about them. Besides the overcrowding resulting from both population growth and a string of cholera epidemics, echoes of earlier days could be heard in the fear that inadequate burials were leading to increased disease and contamination of the water.

Fueling this near panic was the fact that the city morgue, as well as a holding building for epidemic victims, (the so-called Pest House), were both located on the Chicago City Cemetery grounds. By the mid-1850s, concerned congregations and families were beginning to bury their loved ones at "safer" outlying sites such as Graceland, Rosehill, Calvary, and Oak Woods, and by the early 1870s, City Cemetery was closed.

After all the unpleasant lessons had been learned, Chicago went about its business, secure in the belief that Lincoln Park's posh property was virtually corpse-free, except for the tomb of Mr. Couch and the unmarked grave of David Kennison (1736—1852), who claimed to be a 116-year-old Boston Tea Party survivor. But a far different story would someday come to light, after smoldering for generations just under the surface.

During an interview with researcher Pamela Bannos around the year 2000, Lester Fisher, erstwhile director of Lincoln Park Zoo, (which stands on the old cemetery property), talked of a casket being found in 1962 when the foundation was dug for the familiar red barn at the "Farm in the Zoo" exhibit on the zoo's West end. When the City gave no response to requests for direction for dealing with the remains, zoo administration directed the reburial of the remains where they had been found. The remains were reinterred, concrete was poured, and the barn built on top, where it stands (and where the remains lie) today.

In 1970, bones were found during the building of an addition to the Chicago Historical Society (today the Chicago History Museum), at North Avenue and Clark Street. Then, again, in 1998 the remains of 81 corpses were discovered during excavation for the museum's parking lot, just north of the La Salle Street extension to Lake Shore Drive.

Adhering to the Human Skeletal Remains Protection Act, an archaeologist was contacted to work with the museum on a proper excavation of the remains. Archaeologist David Keene found bone fragments in initial soil samples of the area, and so the Illinois Historic Preservation Agency blessed the excavation project with a permit. The excavations were sent to the collections of the Illinois State Museum in Springfield and painstakingly cataloged. The corpses, which all were only partial, were found to belong to 81 different individuals. Along with the skeletons discovered, Keene's team also uncovered a Fisk metallic burial case with a corpse inside.

One of the central reasons for the prevalence of abandoned graves was the destruction of markers in the Great Fire of 1871. At that time, many grave markers were made of wood, (called "head boards."), and history abounds with stories of panicked Chicagoans seeking refuge from the fire in the open graves of the slowly transitioning property, carrying with them their scant but cherished property, which was yet eventually abandoned to the flames.

In *The Great Conflagration*, written immediately after the fire, James W. Sheehan and George P. Upton painted a graphic picture of the devastation at City Cemetery:

> *Into these grave yards many fugitives had fled during that Sunday night and Monday morning. ... The occupants were of all classes. Strong men, hard working able bodied men; weak and delicate women; many of the occupants of fashionable dens of vice; refined and cultivated women; merchants, lawyers and bankers; servant men and women, but the great bulk were the families of small tradesmen, and working people of the neighborhood. Of course there were troops of children, all huddled in groups, with backs to the fire, to protect their eyes from the blinding smoke and consuming heat. Incessantly there fell among them the flying sparks and cinders. In vain did these poor fugitives seek to cover their packages of clothing with sand. The fire would fall upon them and set them ablaze. At last the fire approached them; it seized upon the long wooden sidewalks of the streets beyond, and with the speed of lightning traversed block after block, encircling every place with a cordon of fire.*

The fences one after another caught, the twigs, and scattered lumber, with here and there a house, a stable, or a shed seemed to furnish food enough to carry that fire along. At last it reached the grave yard, the fences caught and blazed; the heat prepared everything for the advancing column of fire. Group after group fled before the flame; the straw beds, chairs, tables, the trunks, the bundles of clothes and the household goods, soon were on fire; head board after head board blazed as a brazen mirror reflecting light. The little fences around the burial lots, the scanty trees and shrubbery all took fire, and each fed the rapacious flames.

The living had to abandon even the desolate grave yard, and the fire swept from the earth everything that was consumable. Stout trees were burned down below the ordinary level of the soil in which they grew. These cemeteries before the fire were desolate— – one half the dead having been disinterred, and the monuments and valuable adornments removed, and now came the fire to make desolation more desolate, not a vestige remains of anything in these silent cities of the dead save the blackened embers of the once erect grave signs, and of the little property carried there for safety and then overtaken and consumed by the insatiable fire.

...There are no strangers here. There are no ceremonies. The cement of a kindred sorrow has done its work. ...At last the raging sea sweeps by to the northward, following the line of houses, and the most reckless or courageous ... lie down upon the graves to sleep— – the queerest camp that ever gathered under heaven.

At two o'clock came the blessed rain . . . .

Ghosts of Lincoln Park

In recent years, artist and researcher Pamela Bannos publicly shared the tireless work she had done for years on the history of City Cemetery. Her expansive "Hidden Truths" project has revealed some staggering discrepancies between the long standing records and beliefs, and the reality of the truth. For generations, historians put the numbers of forgotten graves in Lincoln Park at around one thousand. Bannos discovered that, from the estimated 35,000 burials in City Cemetery (and the adjoining Catholic Cemetery), there were approximately 14,500 disinterments of marked graves, along with about 8,000 bodies from the potter's field, the latter of which were moved to Oak Woods and the Cook County Poor Farm Cemetery (in the Dunning neighborhood).

Left behind, then, in Lincoln Park, would be an estimated 13,000 unmarked graves.

WILD NIGHTS

[2] Lion House old photo via *Library of Congress*

Ghosts of Lincoln Park

3

---

[3] Lion House from Wikimedia Commons:
https://commons.wikimedia.org/wiki/File:Lion_House_%289416126514%29.jpg

4

Ghost hunters have long known of the haunting of these old cemetery grounds by the dead left behind after the Great Fire, but while several investigations have been done on the public grounds of Lincoln Park and in some of the private homes and businesses of the surrounding area, no investigation had ever been done of the Lincoln Park Zoo, which spread from it original enclosure over a large acreage, including much of the former cemetery grounds. When, then, the events manager called me in the spring of 2013 about creating a "ghost tour" of the zoo for patrons as part of its

---

[4] Devil's Toybox Photo by Colleen Nadas

public programming, I was beyond thrilled at the prospect, and we immediately set a date for an initial investigation night.

I knew exactly where I wanted to go on that first visit, because over many years I had been approached via letter, phone call and email about close encounters in, of all places, the women's restroom in the Lion House basement. Time after time, women would report having used the facility and, while washing their hands or applying makeup, seeing in the mirrors men and women dressed in Victorian clothing. On the night of the first investigation that summer, myself and another investigator entered the restroom and were immediately struck by the layout of the room. Rows of sinks lined the two walls, parallel to each other. Above the sinks were rows of mirrors, creating an "infinity" effect from the two walls of mirrors facing each other.

Now, most paranormal investigators will concur that mirrors are one of those things—like salt or water—that have some definite power in the world of the preternatural. Steeped in folklore, these items really do seem to have some importance in the realm of paranormal experience. One theory is that entities can be easily "trapped" in mirrors. Presumably, the spirits enter them to explore the objects they see reflected, but suddenly find themselves engulfed in blackness, on the other side of the mirror's glass—essentially inside the mirror.

This works the opposite way as well. My friend Colleen Nadas, a medium, likes to build and use a tool called "The Devil's Toybox," which is a kind of "ghost trap" comprised of a cube made of inward facing square mirrors, securely taped together at the seams. Investigators use contact microphones to record sounds from inside the box, believing that if a spirit attempts to investigate, it will find itself trapped because of the mirrors and start to make a fuss. Sometimes this "fussing" leads to great electronic voice phenomena, or EVP: recordings of the voices of the angry or frightened ghosts or knocking sounds from inside the box. In the zoo's Lion House, we instantly theorized that entities were routinely finding themselves stuck in these mirrors due to the effect created by the rows of mirrors facing each other.

Anecdotes collected from the Zoo staff confirmed that staff members had also experienced encounters here, especially hearing a man's voice commanding, "Get out!" Amazingly, when I set up my laptop and began to record for EVP, within a minute I picked up a stern male voice warning, "Get out! There's a woman here!" A future visit by a medium confirmed that one of the male spirits had taken on the task of keeping men—dead and alive—out of the women's restroom.

As we continued our investigation, I took several series of photographs down the row of stalls leading to the end of the facility. During investigations, I like to take fifty to one hundred photos or more of each location to see if any of the frames contain an anomaly. When I played back the recording done during this time, I found that one of the male entities was a bit angry that I wasn't paying as much attention to him as the area I was photographing, because he clearly says, "Will you look at me!"

As is typical with most investigators, I asked if there was anything I could do for the entities who remained in this spot. The same voice, now with a tinge of sadness, answered, "Help me...with leaving." When I asked if there was anything the spirits wanted to tell us about their time on Earth, one can make out the sound of a lion's roar and of the same voice saying, "I miss it."

On a subsequent visit to the Lion House bathroom, I was amazed to find that I had photographed a shadowy figure silhouetted against one of the bathroom stalls. This photograph was one of a sequence of sixty I had snapped, one after another in quick sequence. Only this photo showed the image. The other investigators with me attempted to recreate the shadow by standing against the opposite wall, out of view, but could not.

On the first investigation night, after several hours of research and experiment, we decided to call it a night and began to disable and back up our equipment. I would say that, generally, when an investigator ends an investigation and says "Goodbye!" before turning off a recording device, the entities tend to scramble to say more, especially to give more pleas for help. Not so in the case of this location. At least one of the entities was eager to see us go. In response to my invitation, "Is there anything else you'd like to say before we go?" the sound of—perhaps anxious—footfalls can be heard, along with the words, "Turn out the light. Good night!"

My first exposure to primates as a child was at the old "Children's Zoo" at Lincoln Park Zoo: a building next to the Sea Lion pool which focused on education for young children, where my dad would take me as part of our regular "rounds" about the city.

At the Children's Zoo we could watch baby chimps being bottle fed, learn about the varying plumage of birds, and even hold a snake or two. My dad, always the troublemaker, would horrify me by taking off his stocking hat and holding it through the bars of one of the walk-in cages where an active little white headed capuchin was housed. Invariably, the little guy would grab Dad's hat, and a keeper would eventually have to go in and coax the little guy to give it back.

Little did I know while I watched that tiny creature pulling on my dad's cap that Lincoln Park Zoo was one of the most important centers for primate research in the world. Named for a former zoo director and world renowned ape researcher, today the Lester E. Fisher Center for the Study and Conservation of Apes brings together researchers and organizations from around the world.

Dr. Lester Fisher is a familiar name to native Chicagoans born between 1960 and 1975, as the good doctor was a popular fixture on WGN's beloved *Ray Rayner Show*: a morning news show for kids which featured news, weather and sports, comedy and musical sketches, arts and crafts and more. Animals were an important part of the show. Children looked forward to the weekly visits from Chelveston, a white duck who lived at the Animal Kingdom pet shop on Milwaukee Avenue, as Rayner fed the duck and chased him around the studio, trying to get him to jump into a basin of water, which usually ended up with Rayner being much wetter than Chelveston.

Rayner also took occasional "field trips" to Lincoln Park Zoo, in a wonderful segment called "The Ark in the Park." During the segments the host would visit with Dr. Fisher, who would introduce viewers to one of the thousands of breeds housed at the Zoo and talk about their habitats.

Lincoln Park Zoo's Regenstein Center houses the finest collection of endangered apes in the world. Before it was built, the zoo's apes were housed in the modern Great Ape House (completed in 1976), which today is office and meeting space, topped by an enchanting carousel featuring endangered species rather than horses. Previous to the erection of that facility, the great apes made the old primate house their home, which is today called the Helen Brach Primate House. This structure was one of the original zoo buildings but was remodeled in the 1990s to remove the cells and bars and recreate, instead, a two-story faux "jungle" of trees and water, fronted by thick glass and enhanced by an outdoor habitat for the warmer months. The Primate House today is home to monkeys, lemurs, gibbons and tamarins who mesmerize guests for hours with their antics. Perhaps the ghost of my dad's little capuchin is still there, waiting for the tall guy with the hat to come back.

Until the opening of the Great Ape House in 1976, Lester Fisher's office was housed in the Primate House as well. You can still see the door to it, on the left as you enter the beautiful arched entryway to the historic structure. Though he was a famous and much-loved fixture at the zoo, Dr. Fisher's popularity was eclipsed by another familiar of the Primate House: the world-renowned great ape known as Bushman, one of the most famous animals ever held in captivity. Often featured in newsreels, Bushman had been the pet of a Cameroon minister's daughter before being sold to the zoo in 1930 for $3,500, or about $50,000 today.

The cuddly creature she'd called "my sweet little boy" as a child grew into a 550 pound hulk who drew millions of visitors during his tenure at Lincoln

Park Zoo. His massive girth was a shuddering thing to behold. As Cindy Schreuder recalled in her article, "Bushman Comes to Chicago," for the *Chicago Tribune* on December 19, 2007, a contemporary reporter described Bushman:

> *like a nightmare that escaped from darkness into daylight who has exchanged its insubstantial form for 550 pounds of solid flesh. His face is one that might be expected to gloat through the troubled dreams that follow overindulgence. His hand is the kind of thing a sleeper sees reaching for him just before he wakes up screaming.*

But Bushman's real appeal lay not in his ability to terrify, but to charm. Visitors stood for hours watching his antics, which included throwing food and dung at patrons with razor sharp precision. In the fall of 1950 Bushman escaped from his cage, meandering through the primate house for hours until a garter snake scared the giant back to his enclosure.

Earlier that year, an illness which threatened death had caused more than 100,000 visitors to pay their last respects. Bushman survived—briefly—and passed away the next winter, on New Year's Day 1951. His empty cage became a point of pilgrimage for weeks after his death. His enormous frame was preserved by taxidermy and put on permanent display at Chicago's Field Museum of Natural History. In 2013, Winifred Hope, the girl who had loved Bushman like a baby brother during his earliest days in West Africa, visited the specimen in the spring of 2013 at the age of 92.

The emotional and important history of the Primate House made it a definite "to do" on our list of locations to investigate at Lincoln Park Zoo. I especially wanted to see if we could pick up any residual voices in Dr. Fisher's erstwhile office.

Dr. Fisher, of this writing, is very much alive; however, often we find that when someone is passionately tied to a location for many years, their voice, their smell, and even their physical form can leave a lasting impression which can sometimes be picked up by future generations. With his intense connection to the zoo and to primate research here, would we find that Dr. Fisher, upon retirement, had left part of himself behind?

That first night we set up a laptop computer to record for EVP in Fisher's old office space. We left the laptop inside, closing the door and going on to investigate elsewhere. Since we were not trying to communicate with an intelligent entity but simply pick up residual sounds, there was no need for us to remain and ask questions, which is the usual method of collecting EVP from discarnate entities.

Disappointingly, we did not pick up any voices from Fisher's office, but we did find that the laptop had mysteriously ended the recording and started two successive ones—a truly impossible feat with no one in the locked room to stop and start the recording button.

While the recording was going on, we went on to the larger Primate House to investigate. With us was Colleen Nadas, a medium who picked up numerous entities in the building, most of them the energies of children. Fascinatingly, several years later Dave Olson and his group, Chicago Paranormal Investigators, recorded what sounded like a little girl saying, "I want to go to the Lincoln Zoo." During the same investigation, Olson's group was able to record, with a thermal camera, anomalous moving forms along the floor of the corridor.

That same night, I had been recording near the interior part of the entrance and went out into the vestibule to listen to the recording, hoping I'd picked something up. After a few minutes I shut off my laptop because I heard, coming from inside the building, a high pitched screaming which sounded like one of the lemurs shrieking at the top of its lungs. I had several teams with me that night as my guests and thought one of the members was agitating the animals. After several minutes of this relentless screaming, I went to tell the culprit to stop annoying the creature so we wouldn't be asked to leave. As soon as I opened the interior door, the shrieking stopped. To my amazement, I found upon inquiring of the various investigators that not one person had heard the hair curling sounds or picked them up on their recording devices.

Later that evening, I sat on the floor against the wall, recording with my laptop and softly asking questions of any entities which might be present. Asking, "How many are here?" I received the answer, "Many. Like meeeeeee....." And, "We're all here." I then asked, "Are you an animal or a keeper?" In response, a male voice with an Australian accent responded, "Who cares?" When I asked if there were any animals or humans from another country, a voice responded, "I've been so many places." This particular clip is an example of an entity using an investigator's voice to create words, as this voice sounds like mine, but of course with the unnatural rhythm so common to EVP. Very interestingly, another voice mentioned Julie, the events manager who was with us that night. We had all been very, very busy that spring but Julie was eager to set up another investigation so that we could add more material to the Zoo ghost tour that fall. Thanks to her efforts, we finally got everyone together on schedule to come out for an investigation. The entities in the Primate House evidently knew it had been hard to coordinate, because when I asked, "Are you glad we are here?" A voice says, "I love it. Julie caught you."

Of course, in all of the locations investigated, there was the possibility that entities were attached to the bodies who had been interred at the City Cemetery which formerly stood here. During one investigation, Dave Olson and the Chicago Paranormal Investigators asked, "Are you part of the cemetery that was here?" A male voice answered, "Yes, I was."

THE VAMPIRE HUNTERS

THE LAKE VIEW VAMPIRE

SAMUEL PATTON TELLS HOW THE DEMON VISITS HIM.

It Has Followed Him for Many Years—He Has Invented a Glass to Enable Other People to See the Spirit—The Residents of Chicago's Northern Suburb Greatly Excited—Judge Thalstrom Tells How the Evil May Be Averted.

That a Vampire is at large in Lake View there seems no reasonable room to doubt. Mr. Samuel Patton, a reputable mechanic, living at No. 1297 North Paulina street, has indisputable proofs that the Vampire has visited him. Almost everybody in the neighborhood has purchased the glasses which Mr. Patton has specially prepared for watching the Vampire during its nightly wanderings.

---

[5] Lake View Vampire clipping *Chicago Tribune, 1888.*

Ghosts of Lincoln Park

PATTON'S CLAIRVOYIC VARNISH FOR GLASS.

Develops a finer sight that enables a person, when looking through it,
to see objects which are invisible . . .
Specimens sent by mail on receipt of 10 cents.
Address Samuel Patton, 1297 N. Paulina-street, Chicago, Ill.

Intrigued and unnerved was the overwhelming response of the small crowd gathered in Judge Thalstrom's bookshop when the quiet mechanic of Paulina Street passed around his business card on a cool night in September, 1888, in response to the store owner's lecture on vampirism in the modern world. The group had listened intently to Thalstrom's gripping tales before a local lumber mill worker slammed his fist down on the table, calling it all a "humbug!" The others were not so sure, especially after Patton shared his chilling personal tale of being stalked by a vampire in Chicago, after evil spirits had killed his own children.

Patton went on to pass around small pieces of glass which had been coated with the mysterious glaze of his own invention which, he claimed, transformed ordinary glass into spirit detection glass, through which anyone could see invisible entities, including the vampire which he claimed roamed, invisibly, on the desolate corners of 19th century Chicago. Patton lived near the corner of Milwaukee and Paulina, and it was here that he labored at night, making his varnish. He told the men he had developed a sense of premonitions when he was a child growing up in rural Virginia, which had led to a lifetime of torment.

Patton had returned from the Civil War and married. He and his wife had five children, all of whom perished, including the most recent, Willie, just five years old, who reportedly "came out of his grave" a week after he was born, appearing to loved ones. Like many of the time, Patton had sought solace by attending Spiritualist seances, hoping to contact his dead children. "I had no faith in the holy books," he stated, "I wanted facts." In spirit photography and séance manifestations he'd found those facts and he continued to pursue more knowledge of the spirit world wherever he might search for it.

One night, in his Paulina Street cottage, the spirit world came looking for Patton.[6]

> *I felt a stinging sensation on my forehead. The letter 'W' was imprinted there as if with a needle. The name 'Willie Patton' was then formed in about the style of letters that Willie had learned to make before he died. Alter that the spirits wrote messages on my forehead. I understood that the spirits had killed Willie and tortured my other children.*

Patton said that, after a time, he found that these spirit visitors were "made of cones and bubbles." One of the entities would sing as it wrote on the man's forehead, which he'd tried to protect at night with a thick silk covering, to no avail. Night after night, Patton's head would be pierced with some otherworldly instrument, the messages coming and coming, as the spirit's voice sang:

> *Over there*
> *Where all is prayer*
> *I'll sit and swear.*
> *Whoora for me, Whoora for me.*

After much of this torment, said Patton, "they put a vampire on me."

The vampire took human form, sucked at Patton's nostrils and mouth, and followed him when he visited the graves of his children. His forehead, he claimed, began to excrete a poisonous substance, causing havoc in the lives

---

[6] "The Lake View Vampire" *Chicago Tribune,* September 30, 1888, p. 7.

of all who touched it. Some who did so had even committed murder, claimed Patton.

Patton's glass varnish became a reported sensation, with many of the people of Lake View purchasing so as to be aware of vampires who might be stalking nearby. The varnish was especially popular among the community of men who worked at the Harvester Works. When they went out at night, they told their wives upon return of their colleagues' efforts to see Patton's vampire, which he claimed stalked the streets of the north side and the then-suburb of Lake View. Unease reigned among believers, but Patton told them they could protect themselves by sleeping feet to feet with the other members of their households, as he had met some vampires who sucked blood and energy out of the soles of victims' feet.

When the vampire failed to appear through anyone's treated glass, the vampire fervor began to die down. It returned, however, with a vengeance two months later when, in November, Claes Larsen went missing, failing to return home one night. The local barkeep told his wife he'd been there the night before but had been despondent, as if in fear of some impending doom. Neighbors, filled with trepidation, immediately wondered if the Lake View vampire had gotten the beleaguered man, suggesting also that the new houses being built in the area were doomed to be plagued by the vampire and by ghosts. This time, the newspapers were less gentle, sparing no expense in the mockery of the local fears. The *Tribune* wrote that the Lake View Historical Society was conducting interviews with locals for a paper on vampires and runaway husbands, among other jabs.

Larsen's wife—and a good number of neighbors—were not so flippant. After a long night of fretting, Mrs. Larsen went to police to report that her husband had been accosted by a vampire. When police did little to respond rather than take a report, it was said that a local group of boys, none of them older than ten, banded together to find and destroy the creature. Calling themselves the "Vampire Hunters" they trekked through Lincoln Park all day Sunday, searching the City Cemetery for the casket of a slumbering ghoul, egged on by their leader's tales of St. George and the Dragon.

Nightfall had brought no capture, and Mrs. Larsen had nearly given up hope. Then, with a creak of the door, her husband appeared on the step of their Otto Street home, hat in his hands and apologetic for his absence. After his wife's tearful tale of the great Vampire Hunt to save him from destruction, her husband confessed that he had merely been out drinking all night and had passed out and slept off the bender all day.

While no one but Samuel Patton ever saw the Lake View vampire whose reputation briefly terrorized the people of Chicago in 1888, this would not be the last time, amazingly, that a group of children would form a vampire hunting posse. Years later, in Glasgow, a vampire frenzy would break out, causing nearly one hundred children to converge on a local cemetery, armed with rocks and sticks, searching for a vampire with iron teeth who had reportedly strangled and eaten two little boys. As the *Boston Globe* reported:

> *Swarms of grimy-faced urchins scaled the walls around the cemetery in the Gorbals slum area. A group of children, slowly growing into a crowd of hundreds, pushed through the streets to the cemetery to 'kill the vampire.'*
>
> *...Once there, they poured over grave mounds in a yelling, excited throng. Police were called in to clear the cemetery, but bands of youngsters still roamed outside the walls 'hunting the vampire' until dark.*

Ghosts of Lincoln Park

THE SUDDEN STORM

7

It is an interesting coincidence that the bronze monuments in Chicago's Lincoln Park—one of the city's most haunted places—comprise a sort of "supernatural sculpture garden," where one may learn a good deal of the paranormal history of America by strolling through the walkways.

The Lincoln Memorial, behind the Chicago History Museum, commemorates the man who was famously connected in life to a spiritual world through dreams and premonitions, and whose phantom funeral train still pulls into Chicago as May dawns each year, as the real thing did after his assassination in 1865. Each year, around the first of May, trainspotters, Lincoln enthusiasts and others congregate along the tracks or on the Roosevelt Road bridge to watch for the infamous specter, said to be manned by a literal skeleton crew and with a phantom Union guard standing by.

---

[7] Lincoln Memorial *Library of Congress*

They say that if you see the train, time stands still—literally. If you are wearing a timepiece of any kind, it will stop and never work again.

Benjamin Franklin is commemorated in Lincoln Park by a memorial that stands on the north side of the pedestrian tunnel between the museum and the ball fields. When Spiritualism was in its heyday, Franklin's spirit was a frequent guest in séance parlors; believers were convinced that the inventor of the telegraph could also possess the power to communicate across the veil of death.

General Ulysses S. Grant's statue commands the vista over the south pond on the west and Lake Shore Drive on the east, towering over a city that greatly lauded him in life. Few know, however, that Grant was known to have had numerous "presentiments" during his lifetime, including precognition of his becoming head of the American army. His wife, Julia, shared his gifts, even successfully urging her husband to leave town with her on Good Friday, 1865, when they were scheduled to attend a performance of *My American Cousin* at Ford's Theater with President Lincoln.

On the other side of the drive, near the lake shore, a monument to Swedish spiritual philosopher Emmanuel Swedenborg commemorates a man who many call the father of paranormal research, directly influential in the founding of the Society of Psychical Research, and its offshoot, the American Society for Psychical Research.

If you read the previous section, you would understandably assume that the haunting of Lincoln Park and its zoo is wholly the result of the destruction of the City Cemetery by the Great Fire and the abandonment of the more than ten thousand bodies left behind in unmarked graves in its aftermath. But you might be wrong. For it is estimated that, from before the Great Fire until 1919, over one hundred people lost their lives in Lincoln Park, the majority of them the victims of accidental drowning or—most often—of suicide.[8]

On the evening of Saturday, June 16, 1892, thousands of visitors thronged Chicago's pristine Lincoln Park, the city's favorite place for recreation. Though thousands of bodies still slumbered below, the former City Cemetery had long been redeveloped as a lush expanse of manicured gardens, boating ponds and walkways, highlighted by popular zoological gardens and a light-filled plant conservatory, and on any given day Chicagoans came out by the thousands to enjoy the lakefront air and cheerful scenery.

The sun had been particularly hot that Thursday afternoon, and even after 6:00 p.m. its rays drove dozens to seek shade under trees, in the boathouse and under the cool, dark, arched edifice supporting the park's monument to General Ulysses S. Grant—which can still be seen today towering between the park and the lagoon just west of Lake Shore Drive.

Some gathered had sought shelter under the statue, the base of which is a long corridor with arched, open windows overlooking the park to the west and the lake to the east, with stairs leading down to the lagoon.

Just before half past six o'clock in the evening, a sudden storm came up, dense clouds rolling in from the west toward the water. As the fronts met, faint jags of lighting flashed over the distant skies and a summer rain began to fall, sending more running for shelter under the Grant Monument. They crowded together, awaiting the end of the rain, which had become a torrent in a few minutes' time.

---

[8]The Bridge of Sighs

Reports of death in Lincoln Park between 1893 and 1920 are too numerous to reference in a volume such as this. I have included references for only direct quotes used in this section. For each incident included I have tried to indicate the month and year for the reader's further research. All incidents were reported by either the *Inter Ocean* or the *Chicago Tribune*.

Suddenly, without any warning, there was a blinding flash and a massive boom.

A bolt of lightning had struck the left hind leg of the bronze horse on which General Grant is mounted. The current traveled along the northwest corner of the granite coping and hummed into the corridor beneath. In its silent power, all of those huddled below were knocked off their feet. A moment later, some came to—others did not. In all, thirty-seven were injured and three killed in the freak event.

Officer Murphy was on the beat in Lincoln Park that afternoon and told reporters about the scene:

> *I make a run to my box for my rubber coat. I had started from underneath the monument when the bolt descended. I was still within ten feet of the monument. Involuntarily I turned around, and where, a second before I had seen a crowd of 37 people in conversation, I found forty unconscious figures strewn about the stone floor. It was an awful sight. I was fearfully dazed myself, but I hastened in to see if all were dead. Close beside where I had been standing a moment before had stood a young man and woman. He was lying dead at the south end of the second arch and she was making an effort to crawl to his side.*[9]

Officer Duddles was on duty that day as well and called the scene "the most terrible sight…ever witnessed."

> *The people who were least affected by the lightning were making painful attempts to get upon their feet. Some had succeeded, some were crawling about in an aimless way, and four were entirely motionless and apparently dead. In the southeast corner of the north arch was Mrs. Schele the*

---

[9] "People Struck by Lightning in Lincoln Park," *Chicago Tribune*, June 17, 1892, 1.

old lady. She was sitting up against the granite wall, and, with the exception of a dark hue about her cheeks, she was apparently unscathed by the lightning. She, however, had suffered the worst of all by its mad freak. Her clothing was torn in shreds from her shoulders in many places, as if it had been cut with a knife. Strangely enough, her shoes had been torn from her feet, and they lay nearby, ripped and broken. She had evidently been instantly killed. At the time that the lightning struck her she held in her arms the little child of her and William Hulluns. It had escaped without a scratch, and when the wagon arrived it was laughing in its father's arms. Mr. Hulluns had arrived at the monument just a moment before the flash came to take his family home in his carriage. He fortunately escaped injury. Meyer's body was lying in the third archway, prone on its back. He was right in the path of the lightning, and, if there could be such a thing as first, he was the first to be killed. Like the rest, his face and hands had turned to a dark color. His coat was badly torn and his right trouser leg was split from top to bottom. His right shoe had also been torn from his foot. Near Meyer's body lay Miss Louisa Schmidt, and she was vainly endeavoring to make "her sweetheart speak to her."

The bolt made a slight depression in the left leg of the bronze horse, near the hoof, and it chipped a piece of granite the size of a man's hand from the coping. Its course across the arch could be detected by a faint line, and in one place it cut about a pound of mortar out from two of the granite slabs.

On our nighttime walking tours of Lincoln Park, there have been numerous guests who have had strange experiences in the dark corridor where tragedy touched down that summer evening of 1895. Shadow figures are sometimes seen peering from behind the arched openings as visitors approach from the west area of prairie flora surrounding the South Pond. Others are seen leaning on the openings on the east side, gazing over the lagoon and the lake

Ghosts of Lincoln Park

and then vanishing. Zoo and park personnel will speak of similar encounters, and one zoo security guard shared that at times, when he's riding near the monument, strange voices will break into his golf cart's two-way radio: voices saying, "Help me" and "Help us."

THE LAKE MICHIGAN TRIANGLE

It's a well-known mystery in the Great Lakes region of the U.S. that Lake Michigan has its own mysterious triangle, hosting many strange events that seem to mirror those of the famed Bermuda Triangle. While you're visiting the Grant Monument and looking for ghosts of the Sudden Storm, be sure to spend some time there scanning the wide open vista of Lake Michigan for ghostly goings-on.

---

[10] Grant Monument *Library of Congress*

The first mention of strange goings-on in the so-called "Bermuda Triangle" were by Christopher Columbus, who claimed to have experienced a number of the phenomena that would be encountered by Triangle victims in later centuries. Notably, Columbus wrote that the crew had spotted bizarre sea animals and mysterious lights along the Triangle area, hundreds of years before its christening, and reported that, while in the Triangle area, malfunctioning instruments had left them directionless more than once. The modern recognition of the area as "mysterious" first came in 1951, when reporter E.V.W. Jones coined the term "The Devil's Triangle" in an Associated Press report on the disappearances of planes and boats in the area. Over many decades, scores of seacraft and aircraft have vanished from the Triangle, sometimes moments after signaling for mooring or landing.

The Great Lakes have long been known for their own "Triangle-esque" phenomena. Though together known as the Great Lakes Triangle, each of the lakes has its own treacherous, anomalous sector. In Chicago, sailors and pilots are well aware of the dangers of our Lake Michigan Triangle.

The boundaries of the Lake Michigan Triangle run through the lake from the ferry town of Ludington, Michigan, southward to Benton Harbor, Michigan, and from Benton Harbor to the Wisconsin town of Manitowoc, which connects by ferry back across the lake to Ludington. Our own Triangle, like the Bermuda Triangle, is notorious for its mysterious fogs, instrumental disturbances, and ghost ships and planes.

Spirits of the Air

In May 2000, in fact, the problem of ghost planes turning up on radar was covered by no less than the *Chicago Sun-Times*, which interviewed officers of the local controller's union who claimed the FAA was not being honest about the magnitude of the recent issue. At the time, the FAA admitted there had been "thirteen ghost images in the last five weeks rather than the usual eight or nine the FAA would normally expect in this time period." Union officers claimed it was closer to 130.

The next year in early December 2001, a tiny Cessna plane—carrying no less than three licensed pilots with more than fifty-year's experience among them—disappeared over the Triangle while making a leisurely trip from Dayton, Ohio, to Racine, Wisconsin. The Milwaukee Coast Guard assumed the single-engine craft had met its fate by sinking into the lake near Wilmette Harbor, just north of Chicago, but no sign of the craft or the passengers was found.

At the time of the disappearance, older pilots in the area remembered a bizarre incident that had occurred in the summer of 1950, when a commercial airliner left New York for Minneapolis, never to be seen again. Northwestern Airlines flight 2501 would reach the skies above Battle Creek, Michigan, just before midnight before changing course to avoid weather problems in Chicago. Rerouting took the DC-4 over Lake Michigan waters, but as the plane headed northwest towards the Wisconsin border, it simply vanished, and no trace of it would ever be found.

As Above, So Below

Disappearances in the Lake Michigan Triangle occur on the water as well. One of the most puzzling of such cases remains an incident concerning the freighter *O.M. McFarland*; specifically, its captain, George R. Donner, who vanished from his cabin in April 1937, during a haul through the Great Lakes from Erie, Pennsylvania, to Port Washington, Wisconsin.

Because it was only early spring, sheets of ice still glazed much of the upper lakes, and Captain Donner stood watch for seemingly endless hours snaking a breathtaking path through the dangerous waters. When the *McFarland* reached Lake Michigan, crew and captain breathed a sigh of relief and prepared for an easy last leg of the voyage.

Captain Donner went below to rest before reaching Port Washington, but when the second mate went to rouse him as the ship neared port, Donner could not be awakened. Pounding on the locked cabin door brought no response, so the crew eventually forced it open, finding the room empty. All hands searched the ship—in vain. No trace of Donner was ever found, though it was duly noted that the *McFarland* was sailing through the Lake Michigan Triangle when the incident occurred.

Ghost Ships of Lake Michigan

11

---

[11] The Chicora *Library of Congress*

Many ghost ships sail the Great Lakes. Of course, the ill-fated *Edmund Fitzgerald*'s disappearance on Lake Superior is the most infamous, and each December Chicagoans often remember the vanishing of the *Rouse Simmons:* the legendary "Christmas Tree Ship." But while you're scanning the lake from the Grant monument overlook in Lincoln Park, be sure to be on the lookout for another mysterious phantom vessel sailing through the wind from Chicago's past.

Louis Groh, captain of the tug *O.B. Green*, was a well-known Spiritualist who frequently consulted the spirits for advice as he navigated the Great Lakes waters. Like so many Americans of the time, Groh accepted spirit communication—and aid—as part of normal life, a progressive advance that was as much a part of scientific growth as a thousand other advances of the 19th century.

In a *Chicago Tribune* article entitled, "Captain of O.B. Green Aided by Spirits," the captain confided that he and his wife-maintained contact through a sort of turn of the 19th century Skype/GPS tracking service, thanks to the spirits:

> *Why my wife puts them to frequent use. When she mislays anything and cannot find it, she asks the spirits. They write in words of fire just where it is, and sure enough there we find it. We put them to daily use thus in countless ways. ...Often my wife feels worried about me and wants to know just where I am and what I am doing. She calls upon her guiding spirit and asks the question. The spirit goes out and sees me and comes back and tells her, all in the twinkling of an eye. Sometimes even she wants to send a message to me and has no way to do so. She merely calls in spirit, asks to have me told, and knows it is done. The spirit appears to me here and writes the message for me. Sometimes I can see just the hand, tracing the burning letters. I am used to these*

things, and they do not seem at all strange to me though they might to another.[12]

Groh was known for the numerous spirits that populated his vessel, causing a variety of paranormal phenomena on board, and in talking about his long career related numerous stories of mysterious ghost ships that were frequently sighted by crew sailing the Great Lakes and beyond.

The captain was very public about his practice of "trumpeting" séances. A spirit or séance trumpet is a tin or aluminum cone which has traditionally been used in physical mediumship as a means of allowing spirits to communicate with the living. It was during his talk of trumpeting that the captain's attention turned to the vanquished *Chicora*, a beautiful vessel which was regarded as the gem of the Great Lakes when, on January 21, 1895, it disappeared during a voyage from Milwaukee to St. Joseph, Michigan. January 1895 had brought unusually thick ice to the waters of the Great Lakes, and experts theorize that the ice tore holes in the hull as the *Chicora* battled a ruthless gale on its return trip. The vessel was lost, seeming to vanish into thin air.

The disappearance of the *Chicora* was a popular sensation, as many Wisconsin and Michigan residents had traveled on this state-of-the-art vessel to the World's Fair of 1893. Days after the vanishing, barrels of flour began washing up near South Haven, Michigan, forcing loved ones to accept that their hopes should be laid to rest.

After the disappearance, Groh claimed he had been contacted during a trumpet seance by the spirit of a man named John Ericson. Ericson had been a fireman on another vessel, T.T. Morford, which had exploded, leading to Ericson's death. After the *Chicora*'s disappearance, Captain Groh claimed that the spirit of Ericson had promised to help him locate the wreckage of

---

[12] "Spirits in a pilot house," *The Courier*. Waterloo, Iowa. 8 October 1900. Page 6.

the elegant ship with the aid of ghostly knowledge. Through mediumship, Ericson had vowed:

> *I'm coming back to see you again and locate it on paper. But if you pass over the spot before that I'll strike you with a chill and throw you to the floor of the pilot- house so you'll know it's the place.*

Sadly, and despite the unswerving faith of Groh in his spirit friends, the information never came through. To this day, the *Chicora* remains lost under the icy waters of the Great Lakes, though its phantom counterpart still sails. One can only believe that Captain Groh, too, still pilots the ghost tug *O.B. Green*, sailing the routes of time past, out on the Lake Michigan waves

A Sailor's Strange Tale

Kathy Doore is a veteran sailor who has spent many hours on the Great Lakes, many of them engaged in the races that draw thousands of participants each season. It was during a practice sail in preparation for one such race that Doore had what she still calls her "Lake Michigan Triangle" experience. Her truly haunting recollection of that night perfectly captures the physicality and emotionality of the Triangle's spell:

> *July 1978, a perfect night for a sail with seven to ten knot winds, flat seas, and, as it was mid-week, we had the lake to ourselves. I was aboard one of three classic wooden sailboats, part of an active racing fleet that competed every Sunday and practiced several times a week. Around dusk on this sultry July evening, we set sail for what should have been an idyllic cruise; as fate would have it, the gods had something different in mind.*

Not an hour out of port, and quite unexpectedly, a dense fog rapidly descended upon us. Visibility dropped to zero. We became disoriented and feared we'd crash into one another. The winds were erratic, filling the mainsail from two opposing directions, a phenomenon no one had ever experienced before this evening. Suddenly, I was extremely cold. In fact, I was freezing.

I turned to ask my crewmates if they were cold, and to my utter astonishment, they were no longer standing next to me! One moment we had been packed into the tiny cockpit like sardines, and the very next instant, I was alone at the helm. Dumfounded, I called out and located them on the back deck, where it was several degrees warmer. They seemed perplexed and urged me to join them. That's when I noticed that no one was steering the boat.

The captain raised his arms high over his head, gleefully wiggling his hands and fingers in the air, and stated he hadn't been steering for the past ten minutes. Yet not a minute before, I was certain he had been standing behind me at the helm. Draped in dense fog, the vessel began a curious, aquatic dance. Slowly, but deliberately, she turned on her axis, completing three perfect, 360-degree pirouettes, never crossing the wind. Then, just as suddenly as it had appeared, the fog dissipated. To our utter astonishment, we saw the other two boats pirouetting in exactly the same manner. A moment later, we regained control of the vessel and pulled out of the vortex. In unison, all three boats turned and headed for port.

Sailing home over a placid, glass-like sea beneath the newly risen full moon, I found myself enfolded in the tangible presence of my recently deceased father. My crewmates, also, seemed lost in some kind of inexplicable rapture; the only sound was an occasional splash on the rail. We noticed the lead boat enter the anchorage; it had once belonged to our captain, and we knew it well. As we approached the tiny inlet, we found our old mooring empty, the sister ship nowhere in sight. All was quiet. We scanned the horizon for mast movement. We were the only vessel underway.

We couldn't imagine where the other boat could have gone. In fact, there was no place they could go. We set out in search of them but to no avail. A few minutes later, we circled back and were astonished to see that they were not only tied up with sails stowed but were rowing ashore. Nothing added up. Time either stood still or sped up.

After the third boat arrived, we met onshore. This usually boisterous group seemed dazed and wanted nothing more than to go home and go to sleep. It seemed we'd been out for no more than two or perhaps three hours instead of six. It was now well past midnight. As the weeks passed, I realized we couldn't account for a good portion of that evening.

The following Sunday, as we readied ourselves for the big race, I brought up the unusual events from our extraordinary sail. To my utter astonishment, no one would talk about it. Worse yet, they behaved as if nothing out of the ordinary had happened! The vortical winds alone would have given them fodder for years. It became evident that I was the only one in remembrance.

I asked Kathy Doore what she felt when she looked back, now, on the incident that occurred nearly thirty years ago. In retrospect, what happened? Like many witnesses of the various Triangle phenomena—both here in the Great Lakes and in the infamous Bermuda area—Doore believes she and the crew had temporarily "entered a 'parallel reality' from the moment I

Ghosts of Lincoln Park

looked down into the water and called out to my crewmates until we entered port and found the other crew rowing ashore, re-emerging into the present timeline."

The Lake Monster

![Fort Sheridan Generals Quarters]

13

In the late 1890s, Captain Brinkerhoff was one of the most respected officers at Fort Sheridan on Chicago's North Shore, living in one of the most beautiful officers' houses overlooking the vastness of Lake Michigan. One afternoon in the spring of 1893, Brinkerhoff was sitting near a window

---

[13] Fort Sheridan Generals Quarters *Library of Congress*

on the second floor of his home, occasionally looking up from his reading to look out on the water. During one such reverie a black form caught his eye. The object was moving towards the shoreline in the area of his house and, as it came nearer, the captain was shocked to see it dive below the waves and appear again, a minute later. As it continued on this way, he saw that the object was immense in size and that it was—unbelievably—alive.

Brinkerhoff grabbed a telescope and raced out to the bluff below. When he gazed through it out to the Lake, shock washed over him, and he called to Lieutenant Biauvelt who lived in the house next door to come quickly and bring his telescope. Biauvelt joined him a minute later, quizzically. Brinkerhoff pointed out towards the creature, and his colleague had a look. What Biauvelt saw was the most astonishing thing he had ever seen in his years of adventuresome military life. There, in the waters of Lake Michigan, swimming towards shore, was what could only be described as a sea monster.

Its head was enormous and dark, resembling the pointed head of an alligator. The monster appeared to be hurt in some way, ceasing its swimming after several minutes and drifting towards an ice floe. The creature became surrounded by ice and fought to free itself, swimming again towards the spot where the men had first observed it. The body of the monster, the men said, made a perfect letter "s" as it swam away from shore, and then turned back again, eventually disappearing under the waves near Waukegan.

Recently, a sea lion had escaped from Lincoln Park Zoo, and someone suggested that this was the "sea monster" which had been seen by the officers, but they quickly dismissed the idea—reiterating that the creature was of a totally different description.

During the weeks that followed the Fort Sheridan sighting, a flurry of reports descended on local newspaper offices from witnesses claiming to have seen, too, the mysterious and terrifying creature, but after a brief bout of celebrity, the fervor died down.

Ghosts of Lincoln Park

As for Fort Sheridan, though no more was seen of the "Lake Monster," something interesting continued there after that strange afternoon and inspired by the sighting. Distressed by the fantastical tale, and subtly suggesting the witnesses were inebriated, the chaplain of Fort Sheridan persuaded two hundred enlisted men to sign a vow to give up the drink.

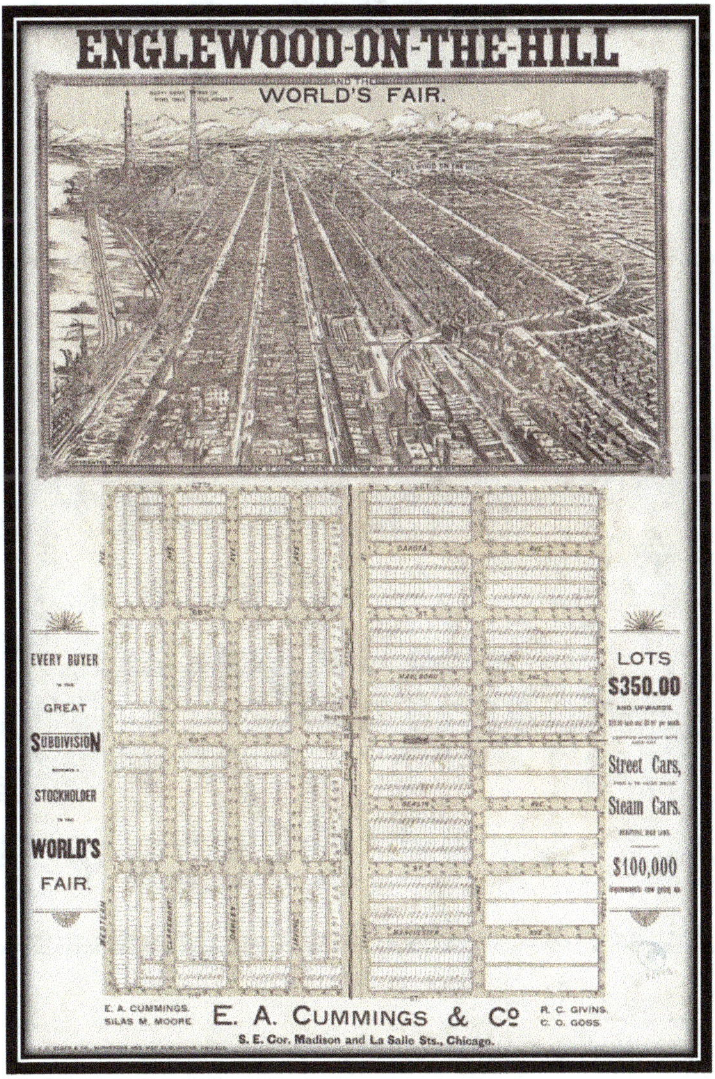

TIES TO THE DEVIL

[14] Real Estate Developer's Drawing of Englewood *Library of Congress* 1890, three years before the World's Fair.

Ghosts of Lincoln Park

15

HOLMES' "CASTLE" (63d St., Chicago, Ill.)

16

---

[15] Holmes *public domain*
[16] Murder Castle *Wikipedia* By Unknown author - [1]/alt source: http://wuapomen.blogspot.com/Published in Geyer, Frank P. The Holmes-Pitezel Case: A History of the Greatest Crime of the Century and of the Search for the Missing Pitezel Children. Philadelphia, 1896., Public Domain, https://commons.wikimedia.org/w/index.php?curid=36506836

Though far from the killer's hunting grounds, Lincoln Park hides a tie to none other than H.H. Holmes—the devilish evildoer known as "America's First Serial Killer." In fact, a major icon of Chicago's World Fair of 1893 made its home here for some time after the Fair came to an end. The Ferris Wheel—a symbol of fun that's been copied by carnivals, fairs and even in permanent cityscapes ever since—was moved to Lincoln Park when the Columbian Exposition closed down. In fact, the commissioners of Lincoln Park incorporated many details of the great World's Fair into Lincoln Park's development, such as electrically-lighted walks, grand gardens and stunning statuary, to give Chicago a sort of permanent "White City" to enjoy. As the years rolled on, few would know they were strolling through a massive cemetery!

It's a dark fact that the memory of that monumental summer of the World's Fair has been forever tainted by the despicable deeds of H. H. Holmes, and even the sight of the Ferris Wheel in its later days here in Lincoln Park brought thoughts not only of thrilling joy but of death. Today, the Ferris Wheel is gone, and the legend of it is a tale for another day (some say pieces of it can still be found!). But the legacy of Holmes and the fair live on.

The sprawling swampland (which would one day border the massive White City of the 1893 World's Fair) was hardly desirable ground for settlers, but when the Great Fire of 1871 leveled the city, Chicagoans moved en masse to the closest unharmed grounds—the outskirts of the victimized metropolis. Englewood became a goal of such exodus, and by 1889 more than one thousand trains passed through Englewood in a single day. But while the area became one of the most desirable in the burgeoning city, it also became the stage for some wild ghostly happenings-some credible and some not so much.

In the summer of 1892 Chicago's First Methodist Church of Englewood was the scene of a ghostly practical joke which even made the papers, when the church organist and an accomplice staged a "haunting" during a young man's organ practice in the gloomy building. Speaking in hushed voices from the depths of the shadows, the conspirators' work sent the young boy fleeing down the stairs and out into the neighborhood. The tale soon spread of the infestation of the church, but the truth of the matter and the "merry laughter" it inspired in the culprits was soon discovered and the full story published to allay the fears of the living.

Less "merry" was the situation in November of 1906, when a Mr. and Mrs. Schumacher disappeared from their Englewood home, a note left behind by John saying he'd killed his wife with an ax. In the days that followed the disappearance, neighbors reported faces at the window of the empty house and mysterious bundles "thrown upon the sidewalk from a window," only to "immediately disappear" on the lawn.

Sensational could be the only word used to describe the supernatural situation which had erupted at the Englewood home of Dr. Louine Hall just weeks before when a series of relentless knockings—always in threes— began on the front door and side windows of the residence which were described by police as "at times loud enough to shake the whole house." As was typical of the time there were often hundreds of spectators who would gather at the scene after word of the knockings hit the street. The disturbances had the entire Englewood police force up in arms. There were reports of shots being fired at fleeing "phantoms," and a flock of "ghost experts" and "spook chasers" turned up at the house to offer their services after a call for help was published in the Chicago papers.

Mrs. Hall told reporters that the knockings began while her husband was away, and that upon relating the incidents he "scoffed at our stories . . .. Next night he was home, and the rappings continued. We tried every means possible to find the cause and failed. Some nights the knocking was omitted; then again it would return. I am no believer in ghosts and would care nothing about the matter, but it has worked on the children's nerves until I am anxious for their sake. I can't get them to go to bed for fright. I think it is some one that wants to be bothersome but can't understand how they do it."

Police standing watch around the house would also hear the knocks "three times, firmly on the front door. Upon opening the door four detectives had gathered from all corners of the yard. They, too, had heard the sound, but declared that no one had approached or left the house. Search lights proved that there were no secret devices by which the noises could be made."

Eventually the knockings ceased, and the disturbances were written off as the work of a prankster (possibly one of the teenage-daughter's suitors), though no one is quite sure this was where credit was due. Could this have been a poltergeist incident? Such outbreaks generally occur around an adolescent or teenaged family member and start and stop with equal seeming randomness. Also typical is the charge of fraud and even attempts of innocent parties to "own" authentic poltergeist disturbances for attention's sake. We will likely never know if the pranksters who received credit for the events actually initiated them or simply took credit for them.

The harrowing events in Englewood seemed to inspire a rash of talk among police officers about phenomena encountered on duty. The next year the *Chicago Tribune* published an extensive article about haunted police stations in Chicago, among them the one at Englewood. A reporter related how, the previous summer, one of the plainclothes officers had been pushed out of his bed by a ghost in the second-floor station bunkroom. The officer had been told by colleagues that "a Polish laborer, who had been killed by an engine on the Rock Island tracks, just back of the station, had taken up its residence in the dormitory... and that it carried a bag filled with brick bats, with which to attack those who came near."

Electing to spend the night alone in the bunkroom to prove the falsehood of the story, the officer turned in for the night on one of the cots. A few minutes later he was alarmed by a thumping sound on the floor beneath the bed.

"Peering out from under the covers to learn the nature of the disturbance, he was startled out of his wits to discover in the corner of the room a life-sized ghost with fire balls for eyes and equipped with the bag of brick bats, just as the other men had described him."

The officer claimed to have been chased out of the station and down Wentworth Avenue by the specter, which hurled bricks after him until he reached his own house.

Today Englewood is a very different place than it was when local pranksters and the "Englewood Spook" turned the enclave upside down, and when police officers had time to play tricks on one another. Most of the posh digs of the once-fashionable settlement have fallen into decay or disappeared altogether, the landscape morphing into one of the most notoriously crime-ridden neighborhoods in Chicago.

Still, haunting tales survive.

Two A-frame brick houses stand on the 6000 block of South Loomis Boulevard which have captured a lot of attention over the years. The houses were designed by a Russian immigrant, architect Carl Shparago, who was commissioned to build them in the early 1930s by a local single woman named Bobbette Austin, who sold them soon after their completion. Chicago Historical Society records show no trace of the peculiar ornamentation on the houses: swastikas.

A couple who lives in one of the houses—6011— says that not only the architectural ornamentation is haunting: the house itself has a ghost. Plagued for years by the sound of footsteps upstairs, the tenants took to actually padlocking the door to the stairwell at night and unlocking it in the morning.

Some believe the entity is the house's former owner, Dr. Walter A. Adams, the city's first black psychiatrist. After an illustrious career (he was head of the psychiatry department at Provident Hospital and a champion of drug rehabilitation), in 1959 Adams fell down the stairs of his Loomis Avenue home, developed a blood clot on his brain from the fall, and died.

Adams' wife remarried and lived in the house with her new husband before selling it to the current owners. Ever since, they have heard the heavy tread of footfalls in the upstairs rooms and hall, and the couple's son once saw a man in a plaid jacket sitting near his upstairs bed.

Not far away, on Yale near 71st street, stands the house where singer Jennifer Hudson's mother and brother were shot to death in October of 2008. Just a few days after the tragedy, Hudson's seven-year-old nephew was also found dead in a car on the city's west side. William Balfour, the ex-husband of Hudson's sister, was sentenced to three consecutive life sentences for the deaths. Neighbors attest that, despite the "free for all" tenor of the neighborhood, the boarded-up house has remained shut tight and undisturbed, with neighborhood thugs even so spooked by it as to remain at bay. Is there some negative energy at this tragic site that affects even the most hardened of locals? So far, no one has been allowed to investigate.

The granddaddy of them all stood on the small block along 63rd street where H. H. Holmes once built his "Castle for Murder." When, in 1887, Herman W. Mudgett (alias H.H. Holmes) was hired as a shopkeeper in a drugstore in Chicago's Englewood neighborhood, he had been officially "missing" for two years. Still a very young man, the not quite 30-year-old Holmes had already substantially ruined his life. About a decade earlier, he had married local girl Clara Lovering and settled down in New York for a time, where he worked as a schoolteacher before hearing the call of higher education. Holmes moved with Clara to Michigan, where he began medical school. The couple's time together was brief, however. Holmes sent his young wife home to her New Hampshire family; soon after, he was thrown out of school for stealing cadavers from the college anatomy lab and criminally charged for using them in insurance scams. He then "disappeared."

A year later Holmes was hired in Englewood, and his boss, a woman by the name of Holden, soon went missing herself. Though family members, friends, and fellow businesspeople were alarmed, Holmes explained that Holden had decided to move to California and had sold the business to him.

Holmes wasted no time in finding a second wife, ignoring the fact that his pending divorce from Clara Lovering was stuck in the legal system and thus, not finalized. His new fiancée, Myrtle Belknap, was the daughter of North Shore big shot John Belknap. Two years after their wedding, Belknap left Holmes. Their marriage had been an odd one at best; Myrtle lived in Wilmette with her family while Holmes continued to live on the city's South Side.

After his second wife's walkout, Holmes began construction of an enormous "hotel" on the property he'd purchased across from the old Holden drugstore. With money from further insurance scams, Holmes raised his Englewood "castle" to awesome heights. Plans for the hotel, however, resembled a funhouse of some sort: the triple-story wonder contained 60 rooms, trap doors, hidden staircases, windowless chambers, laundry chutes accessed from the floors, and a stairway that led to a precipice overlooking the house's back alley.

In only a year, the "World's Fair Hotel" was completed, and its owner sent out word that many of its plentiful rooms would be available to out-of-town visitors to the Columbian Exposition. And so, the horror began.

Detectives and later scholars surmised that a good number of the fair's attendees met gruesome ends at the hands of Holmes in the "hotel" he built as a giant torture chamber. It was later discovered that the building contained walls fitted with blowtorches, gassing devices, and other monstrosities. The basement was furnished with a dissecting table and vats of acid and lime. Alarms in his guest rooms alerted Holmes to escape attempts. Some researchers believe that many were kept prisoner for weeks or months before being killed by their diabolical innkeeper. Others believe Holmes was not really "into" killing, that it was all for the money.

Along with his hotel of horrors, Holmes had other ways of attracting victims. Placing ads in city papers, he offered attractive jobs to attractive young women. Insisting on the top-secret nature of the work, the location, and his own identity, he promised good pay for silence. In the competitive world of turn-of-the-century Chicago, there were many takers.

Far from satiated, Holmes also advertised for a new wife, luring hopeful and destitute girls with his business stature and securing their trust with what must have been an irresistible charm.

After disposing of numerous potential employees and fiancées in his chambers of terror, Holmes decided to seriously find another mate. In 1893, he proposed to Minnie Williams, the daughter of a Texas realty king. Williams shared Holmes's violent nature and lawless attitude. Soon after they met, Williams killed her sister with a chair. Her understanding, empathic fiancé dumped the body into Lake Michigan. Yet, the two were not to live horrifically ever after.

Holmes employees Julia Connor and her daughter, Pearl, were distraught at the news that their boss would be taking a new wife. Julia had been smitten with Holmes at the expense of her own marriage, and she and Pearl had worked with their employer to pull off a number of his insurance swindles. Not long after objecting to the coming union, Julia and Pearl disappeared. When Julia's husband, Ned, came calling for them, Holmes told him that his family had moved to another state. In reality, Julia's alarm over Holmes's imminent marriage stemmed not only from mere longing, but from the fact that she was pregnant with his child. Her death was the result of an abortion that Holmes had performed himself. Stuck with Pearl as an annoying witness, he poisoned the child.

In 1894, the Holmeses went to Colorado with a prostitute from Indiana in tow. Georgianna Yoke had moved to Chicago to start afresh and had answered one of Holmes's marriage ads in a local paper. Introduced as Holmes's cousin, Minnie and Holmes saw the same thing in Yoke: a girl with wealthy parents and a substantial inheritance awaiting her. In Denver, Minnie witnessed her husband's marriage to Yoke, and from there the trio went to Texas, transferred Minnie's property to Holmes, and conducted a few assorted scams.

Not long after, the group returned to Chicago and Minnie and Yoke disappeared. Around the same time, Holmes's secretary, Emmeline Cigrand, was literally stretched to death in the Castle basement along with her visiting fiancé.

Finally, in July of 1894, Holmes was arrested for mortgage fraud. Though his third wife sprung him with their dirty bail money, Holmes had used his short time behind bars to launch yet another scam. Holmes planned to run a big insurance fraud at the expense of early accomplice Ben Pitezel, who had served time for one of their swindles while Holmes had walked away. Hoping to eliminate the possibility of Pitezel's squealing on their earlier capers, Holmes planned to get richer by rubbing the man out. With a seedy lawyer in tow, Holmes killed Pitezel in his Philadelphia patent shop after taking out an insurance policy on Pitezel's life.

When Holmes neglected to pay a share of the winnings to his old cellmate, Marion Hedgepeth (who had helped him plan the swindle), Hedgepeth turned in Holmes's name to a St. Louis cop, who made sure the tip got to Pinkerton agent Frank Geyer.

While Geyer dug up the dirt on Holmes, Holmes was digging graves for fresh victims. After Pitezel's death, Holmes had told his widow, Carrie, that some of Ben's shady dealings had been found out, and that he had therefore gone to New York incognito. Holmes then took Carrie and the Pitezel children under his dubious care. The family did not know their husband and father was dead.

While on the road with Georgianna and the remaining Pitezels, Holmes decided to send Carrie back east to stay with her parents. The Pitezel children were left in the hands of Holmes, who first killed Carrie's son, Howard, in an abandoned Indiana house, and then gassed her daughters after locking them in a trunk while the group was staying in Toronto.

Next, Holmes returned to his first wife Clara and, after explaining that he had had amnesia and mistakenly married another woman, was forgiven.

Whatever devilish plans Holmes had for his first love were thwarted when he was charged with insurance fraud. Holmes pleaded guilty while Frank Geyer searched the castle with police. What they found was astounding: the torture devices, the homemade gas chambers, the shelves of poison and dissection tools, the vats of lime and acid; all revealed the true criminality of the man being held for mere fraud. Evidence of the purpose of the grim house was easy to find: a ball of women's hair was stuffed under the basement stairs, Minnie's watch and dress buttons remained in the furnace; bits of charred bone littered the incinerator. Through the hot summer of 1895, crews worked to unearth and catalog all of the building's debris. Then, in late August, the Murder Castle burned to the ground in a mysterious fire, aided by a series of explosions. A gasoline can verified arson, but no one could tell if it was one of Holmes's many adversaries or the man himself that had done it.

Holmes was sentenced to death in Philadelphia, where he had killed his old accomplice. On May 7, 1896, he was hanged to the relief of a nation and, particularly, Chicago, the city that had unknowingly endured the bulk of his insanity. Some claimed that at the moment of his hanging, Holmes cried out that he was the notorious London butcher, Jack the Ripper. Others swear that when Holmes's neck snapped, a bolt of lightning struck the horizon on the clear spring day.

The fact that Holmes remained alive with a broken neck for nearly 15 minutes after the execution fueled the belief that his evil spirit was too strong to die. Rumors of a Holmes curse abounded during the months and years that followed.

Dr. William Matten, a forensics expert who had testified against Holmes, soon died of unexplained blood poisoning. Next, Holmes's prison superintendent committed suicide. Then, the trial judge and the head coroner were diagnosed with terminal diseases. Not much later, Frank Geyer himself fell mysteriously ill. A priest who had visited Holmes in his holding cell before the execution was found beaten to death in the courtyard of his church, and the jury foreman in the trial was mysteriously electrocuted. Strangest of all was an unexplained fire at the office of the insurance company that had, in the end, done Holmes in. While the entire office was destroyed, untouched were a copy of Holmes's arrest warrant and a packet of photos of Holmes himself.

The eerie string of Holmes-related deaths stretched well into the twentieth century, ending with the 1910 suicide of former employee Pat Quinlan who, many believed, had aided Holmes in his evil enterprises at the Murder Castle. Those close to Quinlan told reporters that the death had been long in coming; for years, they said, Quinlan had been haunted by his past life with Holmes, plagued with insomnia, driven at last to the edge and over. Some still say that it was Holmes himself that had haunted the boy and that the Monster of 63rd Street had finally gone away, taking with him the one person who could reveal all the secret horrors of Holmes's brutal heart.

While the Murder Castle is long gone from the Englewood landscape where H.H. Holmes once walked, his evil spirit seems to inspire the bad seeds scattered in his old neighborhood. While the working-class and the woefully poor struggle to make a life here, others continue Holmes's gruesome tradition, carrying out the serial murders and random slayings that have long plagued the South Side Chicago neighborhood and its bordering areas. Those Englewood residents familiar with the area's dark history may pause at the corner of 63rd and Wallace and wonder about one man's legacy. Chilled by half-remembered rumors and all-too-real headlines, they may hurry home, looking behind and listening, remembering the old neighborhood and the secrets it keeps.

After his capture, Holmes confessed to killing 27 people in his Murder Castle, only a fraction of which police were able to confirm. Many historians, however, believe his brief claim of killing more than one hundred victims was closer to the truth: there are some who believe his victims may have numbered as many as 200 or more.

No excavation of the site was ever done.

During the filming of "The Hauntings of Chicago" for PBS Chicago's station WYCC, our team interviewed postal employees on staff at the Englewood branch of the United States Postal Service, which was built directly adjacent to the Murder Castle property after it was torn down in 1938. Several employees attested to strange goings-on in the building, especially in the basement, which some believe shares a foundational wall of the original Castle, which stood on the corner next to the current post office structure. One employee shared a chilling story of hearing a sound in the basement and poking her head around a corner to see if her colleague was there. She called out to her but heard no answer and saw nothing down the hall, but a row of chairs lined up against the wall. A minute later, when she returned to the hall, the chairs had all been stacked up on top of each other. Other employees have seen the apparitions of a young woman in the building or on the grassy property where the Castle once stood, and the sound of a woman's singing, or humming has also been heard in various parts of the current building.

Most compelling of all have been the experiences of Holmes' own descendent, Jeff Mudgett, who has visited the site numerous times since discovering the gruesome ancestor in his family line. Attempting to make peace with this dreadful reality of his life, Mudgett wrote the book *Bloodstains*—a heartfelt journey through his revelations and remembrances, and his hopes to help heal the family lines of his grandfather's victims.

Mudgett went on to pursue the truth behind his ancestor's chilling death row claim that he was London killer Jack the Ripper. The beginnings of his search are documented in the History Channel's miniseries, "American Ripper," which culminates in the exhumation of Holmes' body from its grave in Holy Cross Cemetery in Lansdowne, Pennsylvania.

Jeff Mudgett is not finished with his search for answers from his ancestor's shrouded story. Part of his plans include the exhumation of the Murder Castle site and the placement of a memorial plaque there, where an untold number of victims died during that matchless Chicago year of triumph and tragedy.

When Jeff first visited the site of the Murder Castle, employees of the Englewood post office told him of the basement, "Don't go down there. It's a terrible, haunted place." Mudgett experienced severe physical and emotional effects from the visit. He says:

> *Before I walked down those steps, I was a non-believer. Absolutely none. I would have walked into any building in the world. An hour later, when I came out, my whole foundation had changed. I was a believer.*

THE THUNDER-MAKER

17

18

---
[17] Totem Pole Lincoln Park *Library of Congress*
[18] J.L. Kraft *Wikimedia Commons* by Unknown author - Kraft Phenix Cheese Foods National Dairy, Public Domain, https://commons.wikimedia.org/w/index.php?curid=107874312

Driving east on Addison Street from Wrigley Field toward Lake Shore Drive, explorers are greeted by an impressive tower of intriguing totems. The "Kwa Ma Rolas," known also as the Kwanusila or "Thunder-Maker" is carved of red cedar and features a thunderbird of a whale, with the whale ridden by a spear-bearing warrior. A sea monster rides the waves beneath them. Since its erection, the pole has provided a meeting place for lakefront visitors and a prime spot for sunbathers.

Bright sunshine notwithstanding, a shadow of mystery has long encircled the artwork. Some observers, comparing photos taken over the years, have alleged that one of the pole's figures, a spear-wielding man riding a whale, has moved. The faithful have cited a native belief in the totem's power to come to life; skeptics have shrugged off the apparent alterations, blaming optical illusion.

Throughout his lifetime, J.L. Kraft frequently visited Alaska and the Pacific Northwest in search of jade and other artifacts to add to his collections. During one such expedition, he came across two totem poles that were thought to have been carved by Haida Indians at the turn of the twentieth century. Kraft bought the totem poles from the British Columbian government in 1926 following a series of negotiations, shipping them to Chicago on flatbed railroad carriages. One of the poles went to Kraft's Wisconsin estate; the other was gifted to Chicago. Dancers dressed as Kwanusila ("the Thunderbird"), and other totems carved into the pole performed at its dedication in June 1929 alongside kids from the nearby Alcott Elementary School.

The pole was not popular with some Chicagoans. In 1972 it was vandalized with paint and set on fire. Someone shot it six times—at close range. Over the years it became so badly damaged that a complete restoration was begun in 1966. Workers from Kraft led the effort; however, the painted symbols were different from the original. There's been talk that Kraft employees may not have fully appreciated the cultural—and spiritual—significance of being thorough in their work. As a result, the original meaning of the markings on the pole faded away nearly entirely. Could it be that this was the beginning of the strange tales that began around the pole? Were the spirits of the totems angered and restless by the lack of respect paid to them?

During research for an exhibition titled "Maritime Peoples of the Arctic and Northwest Coast" in 1982, the Field Museum unearthed fresh information about the totem pole that had been hidden for more than half a century. The Kwakiutl Indians of Vancouver Island, rather than the Haida of the Queen Charlotte Islands, were identified as the pole's carvers by the research team. The Canadian government requested the repatriation of the original totem pole after this discovery, due to preservation concerns for the wood in its outdoor environment. Kwa Ma Rolas went to its new home at the University of British Columbia, but not until Kraft, Inc. commissioned a Kwagulth Indian named Tony Hunt—the great great grandson of the original carver—to bring the pole to his village on Vancouver Island so that it might be used to create a replica. It's this replica which stands in Lincoln Park today, and which is said to represent perfectly the original totems on the original pole.

I've observed that reports of "restless" totems on Lake Shore Drive have stopped since the replica was dedicated.

Ghosts of Lincoln Park

THE BRIDGE OF SIGHS

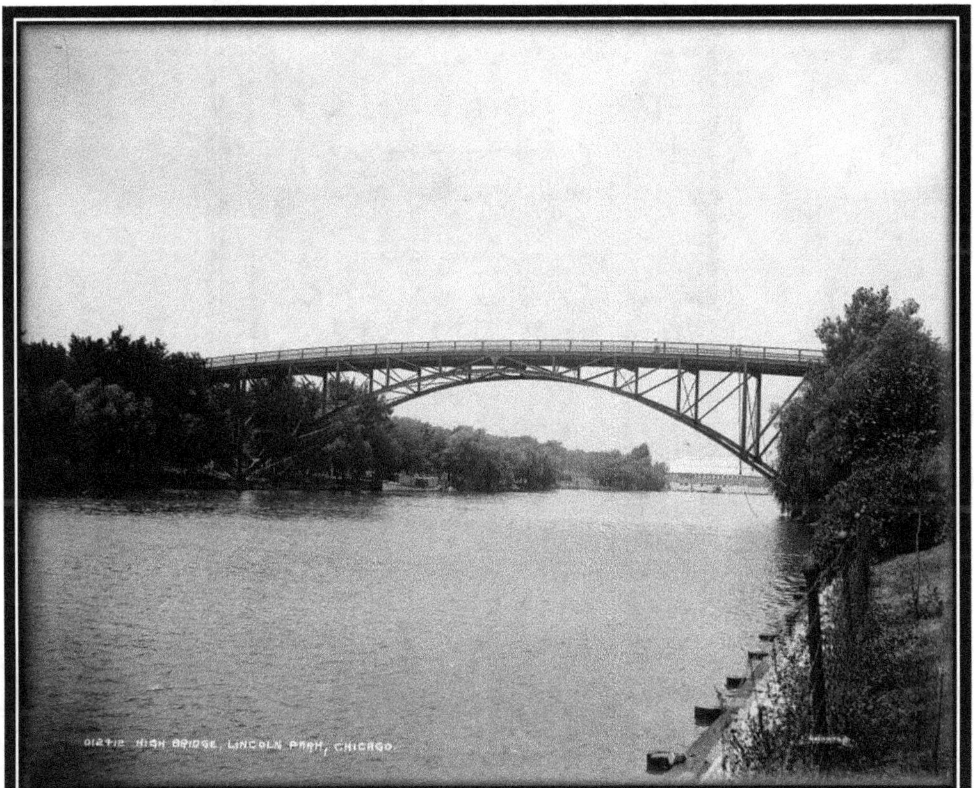

[19] Suicide Bridge *Library of Congress*

20

21

[20] Newspaper story in the *Chicago Inter Ocean* December 9, 1897
[21] Benjamin Franklin Statue in Lincoln Park *Library of Congress*

22

Though the incident of June 1892 was tragic to be sure, and though it seems to have possibly left a supernatural imprint at the site of the tragedy, even this singular sorrow was deeply overshadowed by the many other deaths—accidental and willful—that would occur at Lincoln Park from 1893 to 1919. It was during those years, despite its beauty, that the park became the final destination for many who would accidentally die here—and many more who came here to take their own lives. In fact, it is estimated that, during those years, over one hundred people lost their lives in Lincoln Park.

From its early days, most of the deaths here were of those—mostly children—who met their deaths on the Lake Michigan shore off the park or in the lagoon, which stretches between the park and the lake, just west of

---

[22] Benjamin Franklin Statue in Lincoln Park *Wikimedia Commons*
https://commons.wikimedia.org/wiki/File:Benjamin_Franklin_Statue_in_Lincoln_Park.jpg

today's Lake Shore Drive. Others made their way to the relative tranquility of the park in desperate straits to poison themselves, drown themselves in the lake or one of the park ponds, shoot themselves or otherwise pass from their weariness by their own hands. Most who died by self-inflicted means, however, were the estimated fifty to one hundred souls who jumped—or otherwise did themselves in—from the top of a panoramic steel "high bridge" built over the lagoon in 1893: a walkway that quickly became known as "Suicide Bridge."

Though suicides and drownings had occurred in Lincoln Park before and after the Great Fire, a rash of deaths hit the headlines the year before the building of the bridge. Along with the lighting strike tragedy, a girl named Caroline Wolper, a domestic worker, disappeared from the home of her employers, complaining of headaches. Her body was found in November, badly decomposed on the Lincoln Park shoreline of Lake Michigan.

That same summer, a man walked to the park on an August night and swallowed a bottle of strychnine. He recovered, later telling police that a wound in his head was from attempting to mortally shoot himself the year before.

The following summer, at least three deaths occurred in Lincoln Park, including that of an unidentified woman, aged about fifty-five, found floating in one of the ponds, dressed all in black. Not long after, a dry goods merchant committed suicide by shooting himself in the head at the park after losing all of his property the previous winter.

In the midst of this disturbing trend, the Lincoln Park Commissioners announced, in the summer of 1893, the building of a bridge to span the lagoon and what was quickly becoming a popular carriageway between the lagoon and Lake Michigan—the future Lake Shore Drive. The bridge would be built at the cost of $20,000 and allow strollers to pass between the park and the lakeshore without walking the mile between Fullerton and North Avenues, the only pedestrian ways to the lake. The dimensions of the bridge remain a mystery, with estimates that it was four or five stories high and anywhere from forty to seventy-five feet in height. Photographs from the top of the bridge suggest that it was at least toward the higher end of those estimates, with today's current pedestrian and bike bridge across the Lake Shore Drive a significantly more diminutive structure.

The bridge and other improvements planned for Lincoln Park seem to have been largely inspired by the World's Fair of 1893—which featured lagoons spanned by illuminated bridges, flanked by pristine gardens. I have heard it said that the High Bridge in Lincoln Park was so tall that on fair days, strollers could view the faraway fairgrounds in Jackson Park. Later, after the fair closed, the famed Ferris wheel would be temporarily relocated to Lincoln Park.

Later newspaper reports claimed that the first suicides from the High Bridge began in 1893, soon after its completion and opening. However, I have not yet been able to find any publications documenting these early events. Death did not take a holiday during the bridge building or during the immediate aftermath, however.

In mid-December 1893, probably around the time the bridge was completed, a Russian refugee committed suicide in Lincoln Park after fleeing the czar's army. He had been living in fear of capture, terrified of the punishment that would await. He had been told he would be sent to Siberia for the rest of his life and that his wife and children would be prevented from ever seeing him again.

On June 13, 1894, the body of a man was found in either the lagoon or North Pond near Fullerton Avenue in Lincoln Park. The man turned out to be a Maywood man down on his business luck who had drowned himself.

The next day, a druggist by the name of Mr. Merrill was found near death in Lincoln Park suffering the effects of morphine poisoning. After Merrill died later at Alexian Brothers Hospital, a coroner's jury returned a verdict of "suicide while despondent."

Ghosts of Lincoln Park

In early July 1895, the body of a machinist named John Barnet was found in the lagoon opposite the Grant Monument at about 1:15 a.m. The body was discovered by a police officer on his park rounds when he saw something floating on the moonlit water. He rowed out to the object and discovered the badly decomposed corpse, which he towed to shore. The discovery was the end of a search that had gone on for days, after the dead man's wife received a letter, addressed to "My Dear Wife and Children," in which Barnet expressed affection for his family but an overpowering feeling that, due to his business failures, his life wasn't worth living.

Later that month, a man named John Tris was watching the boat races on the Lincoln Park Lagoon, standing on the bank near the High Bridge. At 3:30 p.m., without warning, Tris jumped into the water. Despite its depth of only five feet, his body did not resurface. A number of men who were waiting their turns to race responded to shouts for help from those who had seen Tris jump. The men dove under the surface to locate his body, a feat that took nearly thirty minutes. When he was finally recovered, Tris was long dead.

The next month, on August 10, 1895, little August Schaefer, eleven, fell into the lagoon and drowned while watching some workmen dig a trench near the boathouse. Later that month, the body of a man, identified as that of John Peterson, was found in the lagoon, a bullet wound in the center of his forehead. The man had gone missing for days from the boarding house where he lodged. On the banks of the lagoon, police found his coat and hat and a revolver with one empty chamber. A recent immigrant, he had been unable to find work.

Less than a week later, Ella Olsen, a twelve-year-old girl, was found floating in the lagoon on a Friday afternoon. The previous day, the girl and her mother, along with another woman, had gone to the park to enjoy a picnic. The girl had run away from their picnic spot toward the High Bridge, intending to view the park from its summit in search of a better site for their lunch. She was not seen again until her body was discovered on the water the following day.

After a year of relative quiet, 1897 brought another epidemic of deaths in Lincoln Park—most suicides but some accidental. In May, three boys were walking along the Lincoln Park Lagoon when one of the boys, Johnnie Scott, tumbled in. His companions attempted to drag the boy out but were startled by the approach of a police officer and fled, dropping the boy back into the water in their retreat, after which he drowned.

In July, in view of dozens of spectators, a man paused at the top of the High Bridge, took off his coat and hat and then leaped to his death in the water below. In the pocket of his coat was a note reading, "Tired of life; no money; no work; no home."

Two days later, a twelve-year-old girl named Annie Schrelber was playing on the lagoon's edge when she slipped and fell, drowning moments later.

Later that year, several took their lives in Lincoln Park, including a woman named Maude Jennings, who jumped from the High Bridge in November after a small quarrel with her mother.

On the last day of the same month, a man named W.A. Clark drowned himself in Lincoln Park after desperate attempts to find work failed. His wife later said that on the morning of his disappearance, he left the house with tears in his eyes.

Barely a week later, in early December 1897, a man named John Schwinen leapt from the High Bridge to crash through ice that had formed early in the season, drowning below the surface.

The day after Schwinen's death, the *Chicago Tribune* reported that the Lincoln Park Commission was discussing what to do about the rash of suicides from the Lincoln Park High Bridge, which distressingly had gained the nickname "Suicide Bridge."[23]

"The last suicide," remarked a reporter, "has called the attention of the Park Commissioners to the unusual favor that their sight-seeing structure seems to afford people searching for a spot to end their lives." One of the commissioners remarked that the number of suicides was relatively small compared to the number of people who enjoyed the bridge, but the commission's secretary said that something had to be done. There had been talk of boarding up the bridge entrances until "this peculiar mania…died out" or of tearing down the bridge. No one seemed to think these measures would stop those bent on killing themselves, but they did believe they would do it elsewhere and "save the reputation of the park."

It wasn't only political leaders who voiced concern over the suicides in Lincoln Park. The next Sunday after the commissioners' meeting, a local pastor preached on "The Fatal Bridge." In his sermon, the Reverend James of the Pilgrim Temple Baptist Church drew lessons from the sensational span, proclaiming:

> *Many of you have walked over it and admired its artistic features and its solidity. And yet persons have used that bridge for their own destruction. So it is that the gospel, which was ordained to be a savior of life, is used by many people as a savior of death unto death. You are horrified at the thought of that beautiful young girl throwing herself from that fatal bridge to a watery death. The country is shocked at the news of that gray-headed man who plunged himself upon the ice below amid the youth skating on its surface. Their physical suicide is horrible, though it is not to be compared with spiritual suicide. But does not a fatality attach to that high bridge? Witness the lives that have been*

---

[23] "May Take Action on Suicides," *Chicago Tribune*, December 10, 1897, 10.

thrown away from it. It is surely rightly named the "fatal bridge."[24]

The bridge suicides were taking another kind of toll as well: a supernatural one. By February 1898, sightings of ghosts were so common in Lincoln Park that the phenomenon was reported in the local papers, one reporter writing that cops on the night watch in the park were asking for transfers because of the strange experiences they were having on duty, both with the ghosts of the High Bridge suicides and others who died before the bridge was built.[25]

A park officer named McCarty was patrolling the zoo grounds one night when he came upon a small park enclosed by a fence. McCarty stopped dead in his tracks and watched as every swing on the playground swung violently back and forth in the wind and two white figures, human in form, glided between them without being struck, their hands waving wildly over their heads.

After his initial shock, the officer jumped the fence to confront the figures, who floated through the park and out of his grasp, over the frozen South Pond and past the statue of Benjamin Franklin, then out toward the High Bridge over the lagoon, disappearing.

Another park officer named Blaul talked about encountering a man robed in Mexican dress, including a wide sombrero, who had "two eyes…like sparks." When Blaul spoke to the figure, he received only a chilling laugh in return. The figure advanced toward the officer and was greeted with gunfire from Blaul. The shots, even at close range, failed to faze the figure, which then disappeared.

Reporters were quick to point out, however, that the ghosts at the park were not necessarily those of the bridge suicides:

---

[24] "His Theme the Fatal Bridge," *Chicago Tribune*, December 13, 1897.
[25] "Visited by Ghosts," *Chicago Tribune*, February 13, 1898, 25.

> *The high bridge, with its haunting memory of unfortunates who from its top have flung themselves to death in the lagoon below, is held responsible by many for the appearances which have made the park at midnight an uncanny tramping ground. Other people say that Lincoln Park in all its parts has been a favorite suicide ground for years, especially a favorite dying ground for people who were discouraged because they could not find work, and that there is no more reason for believing the midnight wanderers are the disembodied spirits of high bridge victims than that they are the ghosts of those who have perished by their own hands in different places from the big hill on the north to the Lincoln monument on the south.*

That spring, things reached an absurd level at the High Bridge, when Paul Tustln, an acrobat, climbed up onto the bridge rail and tumbled backward into the water, performing a series of somersaults before striking the water. Bystanders, unaware of his identity at first, thought this the latest in the epidemic of suicides. In fact, Tustln had performed the feat as a stunt; when he swam to shore after his dive, panicked park goers told him they thought he was trying to kill himself, at which Tustln laughed and said, "In blue tights?" He was arrested for disorderly conduct.

Two months later, a laborer named Louis Rockne jumped from the bridge in front of hundreds of onlookers. In his pocket was a library card and a pawn ticket for his overcoat, which he'd pawned for one dollar.[26]

Not four days later, an unknown man walked through the park gate just north of the Grant Monument and threw himself into the lagoon. It took several hours of grappling to recover the man's body.

That September, a woman named Mrs. A.C. Sagert was found floating in the lake at the east end of the High Bridge. No motive was found for the

---

[26] *Chicago Tribune*, July 22, 1898.

The Bridge of Sighs

apparent suicide; her husband believed the recent hot weather had made her delusional.

More strangeness developed at the bridge that winter when, in January 1899, a woman named Helen Case was found at the top of the High Bridge after disappearing from her home on the South Side. Friends claimed she was under the influence of hypnosis by a spiritualistic medium, though the man denied having put the woman under his power.

After a quiet summer, suicide returned to the park in the fall, when November brought news of an unidentified but well-dressed woman who threw herself into Lake Michigan from the Lincoln Park shore.

Just weeks later, in early December, a woman named Ida Washburn attempted to drown herself and her two small children in the lake after seven years of marital problems. A police officer found her kneeling on the shore. She said she was praying for forgiveness for what she was about to do. She later told authorities, "For seven years I have been a slave to the whims of my husband. He has beaten me until I was unable to move....He beat our children and called them the vilest of names."

In late July 1900, a ten-year-old boy named Willie Ashton was fishing with his family on Lake Michigan's Lincoln Park shoreline when, frustrated by his luck, he made his way to the lagoon to try for fish there. His blue-banded hat was later seen floating on the water by his mother when she went in search of him. Her screams brought police who attempted to calm her, but she refused to believe her child was dead—even after his lifeless body was dragged from the lagoon.

Later that summer, a man shot himself at the Lincoln monument in Lincoln Park, just behind the present-day Chicago History Museum. When he was first seen by a policeman from the East Chicago Avenue Police Station, he was still living and an ambulance was sent for. He was removed to the German Hospital and died shortly after reaching there without regaining consciousness. In his pocket was found a letter addressed to "Nettie," saying, "I have been unable to find employment. I cannot stand this suffering and suspense any longer. Good-by."

By the summer of 1901, the contagion of suicides in Lincoln Park had become a serious concern, with many of the opinion that the waves of suicide were copycat actions resulting from "psychic suggestion" spawned by reports of the acts in the newspapers. In Kansas City, a place suffering its own suicide epidemic, a "ban" on coverage of suicides was suggested, with many urging publishers to downplay suicides in their coverage or to limit coverage of suicides altogether. In response, the chief deputy coroner of Chicago agreed with the tendency for copycatting, remarking:

> *"If I should receive notice of a suicide by drowning today, I would confidently expect at least three more within the week with the same features."* He said the same was the case with incidents of poisoning by carbolic acid, asphyxiation by hanging and other means prevail[ing]. *"If these ghastly things were not published the Idea would not suggest itself to others who are tired of life."* However, he admitted, *"I don't think such a ban could be put on the newspapers of Chicago."*[27]

A period of quiet followed the concerns of summer 1901, though whether this lull reflected a lack of suicides or a lack of their publication is unknown.

Whichever it was, by the following spring, suicide was back in the news when Howard Miller of Keokuk, Iowa, shot himself through the heart at the Lincoln monument. His body was found in the snow on the cold morning of March 30, his pockets stuffed with handwritten quotes from poems about death.

More followed that spring and summer, including a series of three in August. The last of those was of a man named Albert Samuelson, a Larrabee

---

[27] "May Take Action on Suicides," *Chicago Tribune*, December 10, 1897, p. 10.

street tailor whose business had failed. His body was found in the lagoon under the High Bridge; in his pocket a note read, "No friends, no money, no work; better to die."

Later that year, a teenage girl named Salina Peterson walked out of her schoolroom at Northwest Division High School, telling her classmate to "look for the letters…they will explain everything." Her body was found partially embedded in the sand immediately south of the bridge. Among the many notes she had left to family and friends was a letter to her mother reading, "If my body is ever found, my dear mother, bury me in the plainest possible manner, for any magnificence will disturb my rest." Other letters explained that her failure to succeed at school had been too much for her to bear, as her mother had tried so hard to support and encourage her. She wanted, she said, to spare her mother any further suffering over her failures.

The following spring, a well-known high-end realtor named Z.H. Allen walked to Lincoln Park from his North Clark Street home, sat down and swallowed carbolic acid after a period of despondency.

The next year, in September 1904, an electrician named Stanley Ilumason walked to the top of the High Bridge and shot himself in the temple with a revolver.

In August 1905, an elderly man named August Eggers tried to slit his wrists while sitting at the arch of the High Bridge. A widower, it was said he had tired of years of loneliness.

The following spring, Anna Donnenmeyer, a mother of three small children, drowned herself in the Lincoln Park lagoon, despondent over an apparently terminal illness.

Just weeks later, the body of a Michigan man was found under the High Bridge; police could not be sure if his drowning was accidental or willful.

Ghosts of Lincoln Park

That summer, in mid-July, two girls walking through Lincoln Park found a woman's coat with a note pinned to it, reading, "Dear Ed, By the time you receive this I will be resting in the lagoon. I have kept my part of the pact. Be sure to keep yours. FROM YOUR ELLA." No body, however, was recovered.

That fall, in late October, a man named Alexander Evenoff, just twenty-seven, climbed to the top of the High Bridge and shot himself between the eyes.

The following spring, Adam Brewster, forty, tried to jump from the High Bridge after telling a park police officer he was "tired of life." He was promptly arrested.

That summer, in June 1907, two sisters, ten and twelve years old, drowned in the lake off Lincoln Park. The girls' parents believed one had drowned trying to save the other; however, the girls' grandmother told police she believed the girls had committed suicide because of abuse at home.

A month later, a man and his two daughters drowned in the Lincoln Park lagoon. Bystanders believed the man had died trying to save his children, who had fallen in.

A long span of years followed the summer of 1907 without mention of suicides or accidental deaths in Lincoln Park. One can only speculate if they did not occur or if the papers failed to report them.

It would be five years before the next story, when in July 1912 a man named Harry Meyer climbed onto the rail of the High Bridge with an open razor in his hand, "apparently undecided whether to jump or draw the steel blade across his throat." While he decided, a police officer placed him under arrest.

The following winter, in February 1912, a man attempted to take his life by jumping into the lagoon just south of the High Bridge. When he hit the water, however, he changed his mind and began to call for help. Though police sent motorboats to rescue him, by the time boats arrived his body had disappeared below.

After 1912, the record goes dark, with no suicides or deaths recorded until 1919.

That June, a woman named Violet Martin was found, crying, near the Lion House in the Lincoln Park Zoo. "Let me alone….Let me die," she told police, who found her writhing in pain. She had taken bichloride of mercury. Family had committed her to Dunning Asylum, "for no reason," she said. The things she had endured there, a place known for its patients' torments, left death a preferable future. A note on her person said, "I hope I die in peace. I have suffered enough."

The next month, in late July, Bertha Keppler took her two baby daughters from their Hermitage Avenue home and led them to the top of Suicide Bridge. She had left a letter at home to her teenage daughter, reading, "I am tired of everything. My husband has been unkind to me. I am going to end it all." After being stopped by police from jumping with her children in her arms, she told police she had spent her last pennies on biscuits for her daughters, herself "consumed with hunger," before taking them to the bridge, determined to end their constant suffering from want.

This attempted murder-suicide of Bertha Keppler seemed to be the final straw for Chicago. A week later, park commissioners announced the closure of the entrances to the Lincoln Park High Bridge. Suicide Bridge was closed off to public access. Park superintendent John Cannon announced that the bridge was no longer safe and would likely never be used again.

Still, this would not be the end. A final suicide was to come. On September 28, 1919, two months after the closing of the bridge, a man scaled the barricade, walked to the center of the span and dove the sixty feet into the autumnal waters below. It took several hours to find his body with a grappling hook. The man had a red mustache. He wore well-beaten shoes. His name was Edward Hadick.

When Suicide Bridge closed in 1919, many traded reminiscences of the tragedy the bridge had not only seen but also inspired. Stories of love lost, business failed, lives of relentless depression, abuse and violence. Swirling around its dark history were, too, tales of the many accidents and suicides in the lagoon, the lake and Lincoln Park as a whole: the city's former cemetery that had seemed, somehow—to have developed a lust for blood.

Still, as one reporter remarked upon the beginning of the bridge's dismantling:

> *All these episodes are...of yesteryear. The famous arch, which rises forty-two feet above the lagoon, is closed to the happy and the forlorn alike, and the hand of death is upon it. Perhaps it will not even wait for the wrecker. It may heed the whispers of those restless ghosts and disappear, like the house of Usher, into the waters below.*[28]

Incredibly, Suicide Bridge would not go quietly. Devoid of any remaining, willing victims, it tried for one more. On November 15, 1919, an ironworker, Frank Watts, was swept into the Lincoln Park lagoon while working on dismantling the bridge. He was saved by Patrolman William Stift, who jumped into the lagoon and bore him to shore.[29]

---

[28] "Suicide Bridge Falters Toward Ghosts Its Made," *Times Recorder* (Zanesville, OH), October 7, 1919, 3.
[29] "Worker on Suicide Bridge Swept into Lagoon; Saved." *Chicago Tribune*, November 16, 1919, 15.

"...OR WHATEVER IT WAS"

---
[30] St. Michael Church public domain at *Wikimedia Commons*
https://commons.wikimedia.org/wiki/File:St.Michael_1.jpg

Ghosts of Lincoln Park

In the early 1970s, Old Town resident Arlene Zoch was interviewed by the *Chicago Tribune* regarding her experiences as a past resident of two of that neighborhood's many haunted private homes. Although her own experiences in those houses had at times been quite unnerving, Arlene maintained that "(t)he scariest ghost or whatever it was that I've heard about is the one that walked into St. Michael's Church ...."

For at least the past 25 years, rumors have passed from neighborhood to neighborhood about a horrifying incident that occurred at St. Michael's Catholic Church on Cleveland Avenue in the Old Town section of Chicago's North Side. According to Ms. Zoch's 1973 account, the tale was told of the late Fr. "Curly" Miller who had done a number of exorcisms during Arlene's girlhood in St. Michael's parish. One day, as the priest was leaving the church, he noticed an elderly woman following him. As he moved to open the heavy door to allow her passage, he saw that the woman was without feet, bearing instead a pair of hooves, classic evidence of the creature's diabolical origin.

In later years, another episode reported to have taken place at St. Michael's began to gain popularity. In this story, which circulated in that parish throughout the late 1980s, a hooded, hoofed figure was seen in the communion line at Sunday mass, professedly by several members of the congregation. This atrocious violation of communion protocol may be hard to grasp by non-Catholics. It made a dramatic impact, however, on the parishioners of St. Michael's. Even now, the story is possibly one of the least discussed of Chicago's supernatural legends. Echoing the opinion of Arlene Zoch, the thought of it, especially to Catholics, is simply too unsettling.

Where did these stories originate? Fr. Miller's early experience seems as legitimate a report as they come, owing to his previous experiences as an exorcist. Whether looking at his case from a spiritual or psychological point of view, his vision at the rear of St. Michael's may certainly have been some "demon" coming back to haunt him.

Possibly, Fr. Miller's earlier experience led to some phenomenon akin to dubious theories of mass hallucination. Alternately, the congregation present may have collectively interpreted an apparition in accordance with their specific belief system. Most rationally, someone at that mass saw "something," an oddly-dressed congregant, a disfigured or disabled communicant, or the like, and subsequently convinced others present that they had all witnessed something evil. The final theory holds that some fraud was perpetrated on the community to perhaps mock the resident exorcist and his previous testimony, to shock the congregation, or simply to spite the larger Church.

Today, St. Michael's is the church of choice for the upscale population that has almost thoroughly infiltrated the surrounding neighborhood. The adjoining high school has been turned into condominiums and hardly a trace of the old Catholicism remains to remind the young parishioners of the days when the role of the exorcist was an important one, and when it was the exorcist's lot to face some bizarre and frightening realities.

What Fr. Miller saw that day at St. Michael's remains a mystery. Whether later stories of related visions are truth-based is also unresolved. That the rumors stubbornly remain, despite the parish's changing climate is, however, a fact. That they will continue to circulate for many years to come is a distinct probability.

Ghosts of Lincoln Park

THE NIGHT CHICAGO DIED

[31] Bugs Moran in 1930 *Library of Congress*

32

33

---

[32] Pic of Massacre *Library of Congress*
[33] The Massacre site as in 2013: *Wikimedia Commons*:
https://commons.wikimedia.org/wiki/File:Site_of_the_St_Valentines_day_Massacare.jpg

34

Crime buffs eager for a tour of Chicago's gangland attractions are often disappointed by the city's lack of preserved locations. Many of the most notorious sites in the history of Chicago organized crime no longer exist, leaving no evidence but memories of the madness with which they were connected. Gone, for example, is Big Jim Colosimo's restaurant at 2128 South Wabash Avenue where the owner prided himself both on his smoothly-run empire of vice and the "500,000 yards of Spaghetti Always on Hand." Also gone is Sbarbaro and Co. Mortuary, 708 N. Wells Street, which hosted two of the biggest funerals in gangland history: one in November 1924, when Dion O'Banion was carried out the front door in a $10,000 casket; the other in October 1926, after Hymie Weiss was gunned down on the sidewalk across from Holy Name Cathedral.

---

[34] Capone's grave via *Wikimedia Commons*:
https://en.wikipedia.org/wiki/File:Al_Capone%27s_grave.jpg

Ghosts of Lincoln Park

The Four Deuces Saloon, now a vacant lot at 2222 S. Wabash, long ago welcomed Al Brown from Brooklyn to his first Chicago job as the bouncer who would become Alphonse Capone. Later, the Lexington Hotel at 2135 S. Michigan Avenue would serve as the seat of Capone's crime kingdom. Alas, that palace, along with Capone's own fifth floor suite, has also been demolished in recent years.

For organized crime enthusiasts, however, more missed than any of these is the warehouse which stood at 2122 N. Clark Street, where on Valentine's Day 1929, one of the most gruesome multiple homicides in gangland history was committed.

The building nearly eluded description: a one-story red brick structure, 60 feet wide and 120 feet long, tucked between two four-story buildings that in 1929 somewhat towered over the S-M-C Cartage Company garage between them. On the morning of February 14, a sordid group was gathered inside in retreat from a typical snowy Chicago morning. Ex-safecracker Johnny May, having been hired as an auto mechanic by the notorious gangleader, George "Bugs" Moran, was stretched out under a truck fixing a wheel. Living out of a slipshod apartment, May was grateful for the 50 bucks a week he got from Moran to support his wife, six children, and a dog named Highball, who happened to be at work with him that morning, tied to the axle of the truck.

Huddled around a percolating coffee pot on an electric hotplate, shivering in their overcoats and hats, were another half-dozen assorted characters, including Frank and Pete Gusenberg, who were, per Moran's orders, awaiting a truck-full of hijacked whiskey from Detroit. Moran himself was late for the 10:30 a.m. rendezvous. It was a little after the appointed time when he finally ventured out into the 15 below zero cold with Ted Newberry, a gambling concessionaire, headed towards the garage. The Gusenbergs were antsy, anxious to get started on their own part of the scheme, driving two empty trucks back to Detroit to meet a haul of smuggled Canadian whiskey. Their companions, however, were carefree, having been summoned by Moran merely to help unload the trucks when they arrived. Among the harder hearts-Moran's brother-in-law, James Clark; financial whiz, Adam Heyer; and newcomer Al Weinshank-was Reinhardt Schwimmer, a wanna-be of sorts and a young optometrist who had glommed onto Moran after befriending the gangleader at their mutual home, the Parkway Hotel. After that meeting, Schwimmer frequented the North Side warehouse hangout for the thrill of illicit companionship.

None of the group suspected that a police car had pulled up outside the building or knew that Moran, spotting the car upon his approach, had hightailed it back to the Parkway. While Moran's men whiled away the time under the light of a single naked bulb, four men emerged from the car outside, two in police uniforms and two in civilian clothes. The landlady of a neighboring rooming house watched as the men entered the building, then gasped at the clattering explosion of sound that followed a few moments later.

Soon after, four figures emerged, two marched at gunpoint by the two policemen, amid the clamor of a barking dog. After the car pulled away from the curb and headed down Clark Street, neighbors concerned over the still-howling dog, sent a man in to check on the animal. He remained inside only a few moments before reappearing to report on the scene inside.

Moran's men had been lined up against the rear wall of the garage and sprayed by machine guns in careful swoops of fire which targeted first their heads, then their chests, and finally their stomachs. Despite the shower of death, May and Clark had lived, but with their faces nearly blown off by close-range shotgun blasts. Remarkably, Frank Gusenberg had also survived. When Detective Sweeney arrived at the massacre scene, he recognized the face of his boyhood friend on the body of the bullet-riddled Gusenberg. With 14 bullets in his body, Frank had crawled 20 feet from the blood-soaked rear wall, from where he was taken to Alexian Brothers Hospital. There, upon Gusenberg's revival, Sweeney would repeat the question he'd first posed in the garage: "Frank, in God's name what happened? Who shot you?" only to receive Gusenberg's famously hard-boiled response, "Nobody shot me." Still urged by Sweeney to reveal the killers, Gusenberg instead spat out his last words: "I ain't no copper."

But while the law was temporarily baffled as to the source of such brutality, Bugs Moran immediately named its orchestrator. Upon hearing the news of the gruesome deed, he flatly proclaimed, "Only Capone kills like that."

In fact, Al Capone was at that moment in Florida, playing host at a lavish Miami resort. When questioned by one of his guests about his involvement in the Chicago tragedy, Capone curiously but firmly responded that "the only man who kills like that is Bugs Moran." Of the two testimonies, Moran's was right on. Capone had been the brains behind the bloodbath. While some later stories differed on the names of the gunmen, the core team was comprised of Capone's standard slate of executioners.

In 1945, the front of the S-M-C garage was turned into an antique shop by a couple oblivious to the property's infamy. Unfortunately, their doorway was visited more often by crime buffs than by antiquers, the former of which came to the garage in droves from all over the world and eventually forced the disgusted couple to abandon their venture. Later, in the late 1960s, the building was demolished and the 417 rear wall bricks hauled away by George Patey, a Canadian businessman who first built them into a wall of his nightclub, then envisioned them as wonderfully lurid souvenirs, which he promptly sold off to crime buffs. According to rumors, however, anyone who purchased one of the S-M-C bricks was besieged by bad luck, in the form of illness, financial or family ruin, or any of a variety of other maladies. The very structure seemed to have been infused with the powerful negativity of that Valentine's Day.

As did the site.

Five trees dot the otherwise nondescript space, the middle one marking the spot where the rear wall once stood. To this day, an occasional stroller along Clark Street will report hearing violent screams ringing off the fenced-off lot once occupied by the garage that is now part of a nursing home's front lawn. Jason Nhyte and Dave Black of Supernatural Occurrence Studies repeatedly visited the site to investigate well-known allegations of its haunting. On Valentine's Day of 1998 Dave Black finally captured a photograph of an anomalous ring of mist, the only known photograph of its kind from the site.

Moreover, those walking dogs are often puzzled by their pets' curious reaction to this stretch of sidewalk, as their animals either growl or bark furiously at the apparent nothingness or whimper as they crouch away from the iron fence.

Perhaps dogs, known to be more psychically sensitive than most of their masters, are reacting to something unknown to their human companions, a massive surge of energy produced and sustained at the site by the impact of the massacre; a vision of Highball, forever snapping his leash in the aftermath of the bloodbath; or the ringing in their painfully acute ears of the rat-a-tat of Capone's heartless love song, hand-delivered long ago to an unwilling gathering of wallflowers.

Alphonse Capone left long shadows on the city he owned. Some say that, in light of continuing corruption at City Hall and the shady dealings of police brass, Capone still owns Chicago more than half a century after his decidedly inglorious death. Haunted in their own way by the villain's indestructible and international image, recent administrations have led aggressive but covert campaigns to eradicate from the city's face all traces of Capone's kingdom. To the chagrin of crime buffs, Chicago razed, one by one, the accidental memorials to the town's gangland glory, from the Four Deuces Saloon where the Brooklyn boy got his Chi-town start to the garage where he waged the battle that won his war: the S-M-C Cartage Company garage on north Clark Street, where Capone's men carried out the St. Valentine's Day Massacre of 1929.

As any ghosthunter knows, the site of that old garage, now the parking lot of a Chicago Housing Authority hi-rise, still rings with the screams of that freezing Chicago day so long ago. Posh Lincoln Parkers wince as they pass, troubled by the insistent wails that seem to have no source. Others, walking their dogs, are puzzled by the animals' fear of the lot; unfamiliar with the history of the place, they drag their pets past it, annoyed by their frantic barking and whimpering.

But Capone is not here.

Far northwest of the city, all over Elgin and other towns along the winding path of the Fox River, roadhouses and residences tucked into seclusion tell tales of Capone. These are towns full of houses said to be haunted by prostitutes, gamblers, and rumrunners who turned up on the wrong side of Capone . . . and the wrong side of the grave. Houses said to be haunted by Capone himself (who apparently slept in as many Illinois beds as Abraham Lincoln).

But Capone is not here.

In life, Capone stayed always at the center of the action, most notably at the old Lexington Hotel south of Chicago's Loop. From his suite on an upper floor, he ran Chicago and ruined lives. Though he died in his Florida home, where he'd been when he'd "heard" of the St. Valentine's Day Massacre, it was here that he should have returned to spend his eternity. And he did, at least for a while. From the time of his death until the demolition of the building in the 1990s, passers-by on South Michigan Avenue often spotted a glimmering form moving from room to room in the windows of the abandoned hotel. When talk arose of the landmark's razing, more than a few natives, convinced of Al's presence at the place, wondered where Capone would go. Though some modern-day fans hoped he would resurface elsewhere in Chicago, most prayed for a speedy trip, Heaven or Hell-ward, for the hoodlum, tired of the sordid Chicago his memory continued to foster.

Soon after the destruction of the Lexington, the owners of Capone's old pleasure boat, *Duchess III*, experienced a lively new flurry of supernaturalism on the already haunted yacht. Those familiar with the craft's history wondered at the activity: had the boat's erstwhile captain returned to the only helm he had left?

During his reign, Al Capone spent his off-hours indulging in luxurious leisure, hunting and fishing with often great success. The *Duchess III*, named after a particularly enchanting prostitute in Al's employ, was only one in a collection of cruisers that Capone kept up. After a decade of use, the pristine craft gradually deteriorated. When new owners began a tedious restoration of the darkly historic *Duchess*, they discovered a few extra hands onboard: the yacht was definitely haunted. In fact, so frequent are the visual and audio apparitions in one below-deck area, it has been christened the "ghost room." The owners and their guests have heard a baby's wails and a woman's cries and have even viewed a phantom replay of a tempestuous scene: a male figure grabbing a baby from a woman's arms and throwing the child overboard.

Along with the troubling specters, a number of individuals have confronted intense "cold spots" on board the *Duchess*: freezing pockets of air that paralyze the body, even in sweltering heat.

Even from the shore, the ship confounds. Time and again, local fishermen have watched a flame-like light moving among the portholes of the *Duchess* when she was supposedly deserted.

Capone himself was no stranger to the supernatural. Fifteen years before his death, he contacted psychic Alice Britt, pleading for her help in ridding him of a very personal phantom: the ghost of St. Valentine's Day Massacre victim, and "Bugs" Moran's brother-in-law, James Clark, who Capone claimed had been harassing him since Clark's brutal death.

For nearly 20 years, friends and bodyguards witnessed the disturbing interplay between Al and his unseen oppressor. Day and night Capone's weeping could be heard, punctuated by mad begging to be left alone. Sympathetic skeptics reason that the syphilis Al battled in his later years caused his insanity. Surely, they say, this is the source of the "ghost" he imagined: Capone's own guilt made monstrous by disease-inspired hallucinations.

But if this is true, Capone certainly would have been mad, the guilt of the hundreds of deaths he commissioned peopling his mind with an army of apparitions. James Clark was, then, only a representative illusion—or very real indeed.

SWEET HOME CHICAGO

35

They say that life imitates art imitates life, and that's no truer than in this tale.

In the early 2000s I was invited by the Chicago Public Library Foundation to give something like 50 children's programs in three months over the summer. The series took me to just about every neighborhood in Chicago, from West Ridge to Hegwisch and everywhere in between, and I met kids from every cultural, ethnic and economic background. My job was to teach them about Chicago history with my true ghost stories of the city's past. Day

---

[35] Cabrini Green Housing Project in 1998. Camilo Vergara via *Library of Congress*

after hot summer day, after I'd told them my stories, they—deliciously—told me theirs.

I heard from the children in Englewood that, every Halloween night the ghosts of all the people murdered in the neighborhood since the last Halloween rise up out of the Jackson Park lagoon. These creatures have until dawn, they told me, to prey on the living. The kids in Lincoln Park told me about the gunshots you can hear on Clark Street "where Al Capone shot everybody." And it was at the Near North Branch on Division Street, that a group of sweltering eight to twelve year olds told me, "Candyman is for real."

The story of Candyman—the mythical villain who lived in Chicago's notorious and now-vanished Cabrini-Green housing project, has (as they say) taken on a life of its own since the Hollywood film of the same name debuted so long ago now. Some years later, when we started operating our Chicago Hauntings ghost tours, almost every night someone would ask, at the end, "What about Candyman?" After many such nights, we finally put the story on the tour. And that's all I thought it was at first.

A story.

And so, each night I started directing our bus driver to turn right on North Avenue from Clark Street, and then left on Larabee. We'd park at the side of the deserted street, in a perfect place to view the old German church that, as of this writing, still stands at the end of a vast open field. And there, I'd tell that story of the unfortunate young African-American man who suffers a horrible death and lives in infamy as an urban legend, preying on those who don't believe in him.

The son of a slave living in 1890s Chicago, the boy who became Candyman was, according to the legend, gifted with superior artistic talent. A prominent townsman recognized his ability and commissioned the young man to paint a portrait of his daughter. Of course, artist and subject fell in love and the young woman became pregnant, and the irate father called on the men of the town to avenge his daughter's honor. Needing no coaxing, the mob seized the young man and carried him to a field, the future site of Cabrini-Green, where they cut off his right hand with a saw. Then, spotting a nearby beehive, the men broke open the hive, covered the boy with honey and watched as the angry bees stung him to death.

Through some otherworldly mechanism, the young victim became trapped between the real and imagined worlds, where he lives in the figure of a towering, cloaked stalker, with a bloody hook for a hand. As in another urban legend, Candyman won't bother those who fear him, provided of course that they refrain from provocation, provocation which consists predictably of facing a mirror in a darkened room and calling his name five times.

In the film, the legend of Candyman is investigated by a graduate student (played by Virginia Madsen) at the University of Chicago. The unsuspecting young scholar delves into a world where the violence of Cabrini creates a universe where reality and nightmare hopelessly overlap. Confident of her own scholarly superiority over superstition, our would-be sociologist flippantly tests the legend's verity, inevitably provoking her own destruction at the hands of the mythical monster.

The story of Candyman was so brilliantly intertwined with the reality of Cabrini-Green, and the filming was done right on scene in Chicago, including at the Carl Sandburg apartments on the edge of Old Town—where the graduate student lived—and at Cabrini-Green itself. It was inevitable that the film would make a deep impression on just about everyone who saw it, and that it would leave a chilling question in the hearts of most: How, in a place like this, is it possible to distinguish a horror movie from reality?

The horror of Cabrini-Green didn't start when the iconic red and white buildings went up. Long before, the area was known as "Little Hell," and the heart of it was "Death Corner"—West Oak Street and Milton avenue. There, within two decades—between 1910 and 1930—more than a hundred unsolved murders had been committed. At the onset of Prohibition, killings in the neighborhood were up to almost three dozen a year, many of them the result of mob action tied to bootlegging.

It was a long time still coming, but in the mid-1930s, Elizabeth Wood, head of the Metropolitan Housing Council, announced a plan to raze 36 square miles of Chicago to rebuild it, with the help of thousands of out of work laborers. The full project never materialized, but in the early '40s, a good portion of Little Hell was demolished, and the Frances Cabrini Homes rose from the rubble, named for the literally sainted Italian American nun (who also, incidentally, haunts Chicago). The low-rise townhouses were low-income housing, but the application process was tough. Only United States citizens could apply, and even those must be living in family units with children under the age of seventeen. No criminals, bad credit, or anti-social tendencies would be entertained for tenancy. In other words, few from "Little Hell" need apply. Later, Wood would tell the federal government that they were too poor to live in low-income housing.

They couldn't make the rent.

After World War II, more buildings went up, but these were high-rise apartments, and by the early 1960s, "Cabrini-Green" was a massive complex consisting of more than 3,500 units, most of which were still housing families not from the neighborhood and who made enough money to pay a reasonable rent.

There are probably as many theories about what happened to Cabrini-Green as there were apartments in those iconic towers. Most agree that housing so many people under one roof—with economic stress and gangs so prevalent for most in the area —was a foolish idea. Indeed, the low rise units enjoyed significantly fewer problems as the years passed. The real trouble, however, seemed to have begun with the assassination of Martin Luther King, Jr., at a time when the majority of Cabrini's residents were now Black. Two years later, a Cabrini-Green sniper killed two Chicago police officers. Soon after, gangs began to grow with a vengeance, dividing themselves into the Reds and the Whites (for the different colored buildings of the project), and they ruled day and night, to the point where, in 1982, former mayor Jane Byrne moved into one of the units herself, both to show solidarity and to try to quell some of the violence. It accomplished little and didn't last long. Later that decade, the Chicago Housing Authority brought in Vince Lane as its executive director. He began a program of sweeps to eliminate drugs and dealers from Cabrini, but the patrols were expensive in both police time and city money.

The killing of 7 year old Dantrell Davis in the fall of 1992 was a loud and clear signal that things could not go on as they had for so long. Davis was walking to school across the street from their Cabrini apartment, holding his mom's hand, when he was shot by a stray bullet presumably discharged by a gang member. Davis' death came at about the same time as a Federal Housing and Urban Development program was focusing attention—and cash—on the problem of modern housing. When the Chicago Housing Authority received a grant from the so-called HOPE program, it was decided immediately that it would go to the problem of Cabrini-Green. Most of that grant money had still not been used twenty years later. One of the biggest issues was a haunting one from the neighborhood's long-ago past. Only a scant fraction of the proposed new development would go to extremely low income tenants.

As the new millennium turned, most of the real hope would come not from the HOPE grant but from private developers who introduced mixed-income housing communities skirting the old Cabrini-Green site, including Old Town Village West and North Town Village, the latter offering 50 percent market-rate rental and ownership units, 20 percent subsidized units and a full 30 percent for former Cabrini residents. In an area where townhouses can sell for well over one million dollars, this was a radical development indeed. But available units are woefully below any ability of the city to, as Mayor Richard M. Daley promised, return to the neighborhood anyone who had to leave with the demolition of Cabrini-Green. There is much more to this convoluted story, as much of a horror story as anything from Clive Barker.

Ghosts of Lincoln Park

The culture of Cabrini-Green and the real horrors of life there—despite a strong sense of community that couldn't be shaken—made the film *Candyman* a powerful one. But, as so many of our tour guests wanted to know, was any of the *story* true? Was Candyman a real person, and did the things in the movie really happen?

Well that's a long . . . story.

The screenplay for the film *Candyman* was written by Bernard Rose and based on a short story by Clive Barker called "The Forbidden." The plot of the story is similar to that of the film: a young woman becomes part of the urban legends surrounding a graffiti-covered housing project when she goes in search of the secret truths behind them. Barker was from the English city of Liverpool, and he set his story in urban England—not Chicago, and definitely not Cabrini-Green. That was Rose's idea. It was also Rose who made Candyman Black, and some have suggested he did this because he felt this would make him automatically scarier to white audiences, but this wasn't true.

Rose had come to Chicago to see if it would be a good fit for the film (Chicago, as you may know, is very hospitable to filmmakers, going back to when the Blues Brothers tore up the town with the full blessing of then Mayor Jane Byrne). Rose was deeply affected by the social fabric of Chicago, especially Cabrini-Green. He chose the site before he created his version of Candyman. Of course, as he told *New Musical Express*, now Candyman would have to be Black: "There was no way it could be a white guy. It just wouldn't make any sense whatsoever."

I did find out some very interesting things while searching for a real-life Candyman. First, there was a serial killer who became known as the Candy Man who abducted, tortured, and killed at least twenty-eight young men in Texas during the early 1970s. Dean Arnold Corll's family had formerly owned a candy factory in the Houston area, and Corll had a practice of handing out candy to kids, earning him the nickname.

Before I found out about Rose's process in making Candyman an African American character, I found out something else intriguing. In England, where both Clive Barker and Bernard Rose had grown up, there had been something like a real-life version of Candyman on the prowl starting during their youths..

In the late 1970s and early 1980s, reportedly hundreds of police reports were made in the Liverpool area (where Barker was raised during the same time period) by young men and boys complaining of a tall, muscular Black man with skin that appeared to have a dark purple hue. In fact, they had a nickname for him: Purple Aki. According to their reports, Purple Aki assaulted or sodomized his victims, often asking if he could touch their muscles beforehand. Some claimed they had seen him shot, stabbed or drowned, but that he'd come back. He wouldn't die. Others claimed adults couldn't see him. According to legend, the fear of Purple Aki was so intense in the early 1980s that young boys weren't allowed to work paper routes, and no young male ever walked alone outside after dark.

Then, in June of 1986, a 16-year-old boy named Gary Kelly was electrocuted after falling onto the tracks at the New Brighton railway station. Bystanders told police he was running away from a pursuer, who was later jailed. When the image of the accused, Akinwale Arobieke, appeared on the news, hundreds of men came forward to identify the man as "Purple Aki," the mysterious figure who had assaulted them, and the figure who had lived for a decade as a Liverpudlian folktale.

Arobieke was convicted of manslaughter but appealed and won. He was also awarded a substantial compensation for alleged racial elements in the earlier trial. But, as they all had said, Purple Aki would not die.

In late 2001, Arobieke was back in court, charged with harassing and assaulting a total of 14 teenaged boys between 1995 and 2000. He was convicted but released two years later and almost immediately arrested again. During the ensuing trial, more than 120 people were interviewed by police. Arobieke was given six years after pleading guilty to 15 counts of harassment and witness intimidation. His file contained an additional 61 counts. The judge in the case, Edward Slinger, called his behavior "both strange and obsessive."

After his release, Arobieke continued to end up back in jail, and in court. During a later day in court, Arobieke apologized to his victims and admitted that he was "infamous, notorious, everything from a bogeyman to whatever." In 2021, a video appeared on social media showing alleged gang members shooting fireworks at Arobieke's head as he walks, unflinching.

Did a childhood fear of Liverpool's very real "bogeyman" make its way into the character of Candyman? Was Barker, who grew up with the legend in Liverpool, or Rose, who grew up in London, unconsciously influenced to include elements of the larger-than-life character in the now-classic tale?

THE MAGIC HEDGE

36

Like the rest of Lincoln Park, the section of public lakefront area sprawling between Waveland and Montrose Avenues has become a popular recreational area, both for residents of the adjacent Lakeview and Buena Park neighborhoods and for those that come there on nice days by foot, car, bike, or rollerblade, many for tennis or golf or for softball games at the Waveland Avenue facilities, fewer to catch sight of the strays that wander from the city's bird sanctuary in the woods beyond the ball field.

---

[36] Montrose Point: Shot of the Magic Hedge by James Andrews via Canva Pro

Ghosts of Lincoln Park

With its sparsely used beach, Montrose Point serves its own free spirits, many of them Hispanic-Americans from nearby Uptown who transform the wide lawns of the Montrose Harbor area into soccer fields, and retirees who fish off the pier from early morning to dusk. Later in this book we'll talk about the mystical history of Cricket Hill, the sledding hill here that has been popular for generations of Chicagoans.

But all has not always been fun and games here.

Shortly after World War II, the Chicago Park District leased Montrose Point to the United States Army for one dollar a year, so the latter might develop a military post to watch for Russian invasions. The Army first established a gunsite, then replaced it with a Nike missile site. Nearly 300 men were stationed here, with barracks, a mess hall, a radar station, officers' quarters, and other facilities.

As with any military base, the staff of Montrose Point came from all over the country. As with any such situation, most of the servicemen got along. At times, however, tempers flared. And sometimes, they stayed that way, arguments leading to clashes, fists, and worse. James Landing, a professor at the University of Illinois at Chicago, first shared with me many years ago a now-classic ghost story of those Cold War times at Montrose and the lake:

> *According to eyewitness accounts, of which there are only a few left, one Halloween evening two soldiers got into a heated argument. One was a young European immigrant from Massachusetts named Pique Nerjee, and the other was a southern cotton farm worker born in Puerto Rico named Hernando Cortez Rodrickkez. The argument became so heated that Rodrickkez threatened to kill Pique. Pique remained in the barracks afterward, since he was on duty that night, but Hernando left the barracks at about 9 p.m., since he had been invited to a masked ball and Halloween party at the national office of the W.C.T.U. in Evanston. Based on later Army reports, a strange noise was heard in*

the barracks around 12 a.m., enough to cause the men to get up and look around. It was only later that they noticed that Pique did not rise, and when they checked, he appeared dead.

When the coroner arrived to investigate, suddenly Hernando rushed into the barracks shouting, "Pique, Pique, please Pique." It seemed that Hernando had heard the same noise at the party and, like a man obsessed, told everyone that he had to return to his post immediately. After they took Pique's body away, Hernando ran out of the barracks, moaning and wailing, "Pique, Pique, please Pique."

The soldiers followed, but the night had become misty and fogged and, had it not been for a full moon, they would have seen nothing. Although they heard the moaning and wailing all night, they could not find Hernando, and he was, in fact, never seen again. The Army pronounced him dead (he was believed to have jumped into the freezing autumn waters of Lake Michigan) and reported Pique dead of a sudden heart attack.

The incident was soon forgotten but, the following Halloween night, soldiers in the barracks saw strange figures walking through the shrubs along the barracks (the area known today as "The Magic Hedge"), grabbed their rifles and tried to intercept the intruders.

Nothing!

Each time they returned to the barracks, the strange figures began moving through the shrubs. One time they listened carefully and heard a low moan and wail that sounded something like, "Pique, Pique, please Pique," and that is what was reported to their commanding officer.

Ghosts of Lincoln Park

By the next Halloween the Nike missile site had been removed, but two homeless men sleeping in the park told police that all night "vampire bats" had kept attacking them, whispering that they wanted to suck their blood. Birders dismissed these stories, concluding that the so-called vampire bats were probably owls, and that the wails and moans were the shrieking of the prey they caught, like rabbits and rats.

And so, the explanation went—until about five years ago, when some construction workers at Montrose, doing emergency night sewer work, were distracted by a strange light running through the Magic Hedge. They checked but found nothing more, although they did report a low moaning and wailing of words that they described to their superiors as

'Pique, Pique, please Pique!'

THE SPELL OF CRICKET HILL

Before you leave the Magic Hedge/Montrose Point area, be sure to climb the small but iconic hill nearby.

Many years ago now I wrote a poem called "Leaving Cricket Hill" after my then-boyfriend—an Edgewater kid from the local neighborhood—took me to the modest sledding hill at Montrose Point one summer night. It was an experience I've never forgotten: one of *those* moments where you feel the unmistakable truth of something greater than yourself. There was something intangible yet almost—almost—palpable about the place. It was a soft, warm night. A slight breeze swirled around us as we climbed the hill at dusk. Small groups of people played music and sang; the sound of a guitar, a pennywhistle, a barely perceptible drum keeping pace with our steps up the grassy summit. We met a blind man who walked dogs for a living—a bizarre concept back then. The lake spread out to the east in the moonlight. I was, as they say, taken with the place.

I soon found out I wasn't alone. As I researched it, I found this little sledding hill I'd loved as a child growing up in the not-far-off neighborhood of Northcenter had somehow become a mecca for seekers of the spiritual across ages, races, ethnicities and cultures. The Peace and Music Festival, which began in the 1980s, has surely been a big part of creating the Cricket Hill "vibe." Along with African and other ethnic music and cultural fests, Native Americans hold pow-wows here. The "non-partisan, non-political" FreeFest joined in, with singers, poets and speakers from psychedelic to punk and everything in between. In August of 1995, thousands gathered in the misty air to sing Grateful Dead songs, mourning the passing of Jerry Garcia. In recent years, I read on a warlock's website that Cricket Hill was chosen to be the center of some nationwide crystal matrix, presumably creating an ethereal web of energy for some esoteric purpose.

There's regular stuff that goes on here, too. The soccer fields are—there is not another word for it—awash with players on the weekends. The Hill is the site of the annual Chicago Kids and Kites Festival, which used to include a candy drop. Fun runs are almost constantly winding through the lakefront roads and trails. And always, with the snow, the sledders return. In my own family, each New Year's Day that we wake to snow, off we go.

No one is quite sure where Cricket Hill got its name. Some say that, in spring, the hill used to be covered with the jumping little guys, rejoicing in the sunshine with their spring-feverish human friends. Others seem to remember their granddads (or maybe it was great-granddad?) talking about a cricket field here where English immigrants used to gather, and it's true. The Chicago Cricket Club did play their games on the green at Montrose Point.

Some have a much more fanciful explanation for the naming of this popular hill. As the story goes, the Ringling Brothers circus train was on its way to its winter quarters in Baraboo, Wisconsin one fall morning. Tragically, the train was struck by a runaway engine; three elephants died in the disaster. Two, the story claims, were buried in a cemetery nearby, but the third elephant, named Cricket, had to be interred elsewhere due to lack of space in the burial ground. Here, the story gets a little seedy. A driver was instructed to take Cricket's body to another North Side cemetery, but he got lost and found himself at Montrose Point, where he got talking with a couple of lifeguards at the beach. Instead of getting directions to the cemetery as he had planned, the driver joined the lifeguards—who had just finished their shift—in a shot and a beer at an Uptown tavern. Stories and glasses piled up, and soon it was closing time. But when the driver returned to his truck, they found that someone had dumped the elephant into a sinkhole near the beach. As the years went on, visitors to the beach paid their respects to

Cricket by dumping sand buckets full of dirt onto the poor elephant's grave. Thus, Cricket Hill rose on the Montrose Point green.

This creative tale must have been concocted by a bored lifeguard one drowsy day. No circus train wreck occurred in Chicago; no Ringling wreck in Illinois (it's the Ringling Brothers Circus that wintered in Baraboo). But of course, the Cricket Hill tale includes many motifs from the story of the terrible Hagenbeck-Wallace circus train wreck that happened in Northwest Indiana in 1918. Legend erroneously holds that elephants who died in the wreck were buried at the cemetery in Forest Park, just west of Chicago. And certainly both the nearby Burlington railroad up to Wisconsin as well as plentiful local cemeteries add to the realism of the Cricket Hill tale.

Those who grew up in the neighborhood don't remember it as Cricket Hill but Crooked Hill. The jagged line through the middle, they say, was caused by a lightning strike back in the day. They'd ride their bikes up and down that line all day in the hot summer sun.

Before Cricket Hill, they remember, this place was called "the Jungle." In the middle of the wide green here was a tangle of sumac trees and other thick flora. The jungle extended west past the viaducts, in some places as far as a block back. The jungle was the home of hobos, drunks, and perverts. Local kids knew to never go into the jungle alone, as one or another of these lost souls would invariably invite the young boys into the thick.

Some say it was this kind of thing that led the city to level the Jungle, including the biggest concentration of shrubbery at Cricket Field. More than one old timer holds the magical hill is actually a garbage dump—built up by dumping trash at that site and covering it with more and more dirt over the years.

Despite such unromantic backstories, there remains something decidedly ... elevated about this seemingly ordinary little hill. A few months ago I was contacted by a woman who had attended school at St. Mary of the Lake school on Sheridan Road, just a few blocks from Lake Michigan. While in eighth grade, on All Souls' Day of 1960, she had a most unusual experience at Cricket Hill:

> *Since (it) was a Holy Day, we were out of school. My friend and I, along with her aunt and mother decided to walk to the park (Clarendon Park) which was only a couple blocks east. As we were walking the path, my friend and I... started running toward Cricket Hill, and as we approached we saw "hooded monks" going up the side of the hill (north to south). As we continued we noticed how they seemed to glide. The first one had reached the top and the rest followed, gliding on air. Of course it scared the —— out of us, and we ran back toward her mom and aunt. As we reached them, they too had noticed that they could see clearly from the ground to the end of their robes. I remember they had the hoods up and appeared to have their hands folded in prayer.*

CURTAINS FOR A DIRTY RAT

37

38

---

[37] John Dillinger: FBI photo (public domain)
[38] Baby Face Nelson FBI photo (public domain)

39

The focal point in the thrilling tale that created one of the city's most famous and favorite ghosts, the Biograph Theater on north Lincoln Avenue welcomed a very special guest on a hot July night in 1934 to his last picture show: John Dillinger, christened by his pursuers as Public Enemy Number One.

That evening, Dillinger left the theater accompanied by Anna Sage, the legendary "Lady in Red" and a favorite prostitute, Polly Hamilton, with whom he had been holed up with at her 2420 N. Halsted Street apartment. At that point, the infamous criminal met his long-avoided end in a narrow alleyway just steps from the theater doors. The bullet fired through the back of his neck by FBI Agent Charles Winstead had been a long time coming.

---

[39] Biograph Theater: Photo of theater after Dillinger's shooting. Note the sign advertising souvenir photos inside of Dillinger's movie seat. FBI photo (public domain).

Curtains for a Dirty Rat

Congratulations poured into the Chicago Police Department and U.S. government agencies from around the world. For while Dillinger's international renown had been quickly won, he made it unforgettable by being impossibly hard to nab. For four months, Melvin Purvis, the soft-spoken head of Chicago's FBI agents, had lived and breathed the chase for the Indiana-born gangster, desperate to snag him before Purvis' critics could oust him in favor of "a more experienced man." In hot pursuit of his prey, Purvis had lived from tip to tip, leading his agents in a foiled attempt to surround the scoundrel at a State Street and Austin cafe, an impressive but ill-fated attack on Dillinger's North Woods hideout at Sault St. Marie, and the infamous confrontation at Wisconsin's Little Bohemia Lodge, in which FBI agents recklessly injured two civilians and killed a third. It was here, too, that George "Baby Face" Nelson reportedly killed Special Agent W. Carter Baum, prompting FBI Chief J. Edgar Hoover to call Nelson a "rat."

Yet these near misses with the FBI were only the last stretch of a sensational, though short, career. Summary of the "High Points in Life of John Dillinger" was provided by the *Chicago Tribune* on the morning after his fatal shooting. What follows the headline is a catalog of arrests, sentencings, shootouts, and escapes. At the age of 20, Dillinger held up his hometown grocery store in Mooresville, Indiana. Pleading guilty, he was sentenced to serve 10 to 20 years in prison, while his accomplice, pleading not guilty, received a sentence of little more than two years. Bitterly reflecting on this joke of justice, Dillinger spent a quiet eight and a half years planning his revenge on the law. On May 22, 1933, the then-unknown Dillinger was paroled and proceeded to rob three banks in as many months, making off with $40,000. He was incarcerated at Lima, Ohio in September of that same year. When, barely three weeks later, three former fellow inmates invaded the prison and sprung Dillinger, they ushered the convict into a brief but stellar stint as an internationally notorious gangster. His gang would be described after his death as "the most notorious band of outlaws in America, probably the world."

Eluding a police trap in November, the gang pulled off a bank robbery later that month. To celebrate the new year, an unrepentant Dillinger shot and killed police officer William O'Malley in another bank robbery in East Chicago, for which he was arrested in Arizona and sent to Crown Point, Indiana to stand trial. Predictably, he escaped a month later by carving a gun out of soap and blackening it with shoe polish and eluded pursuers for another month. Finding himself at that point in another jam, he shot his way out of a St. Paul police trap on March 31st and made a similar escape from the FBI trap near Mercer, Wisconsin, where he killed two people in the process at the Little Bohemia Lodge. Two months later, police found a Ford V-8 at Roscoe and Leavitt streets treated with a fingerprint-dissolving chemical and with one of the windows smashed out to facilitate shotgunning. Inside the car were a half dozen pop bottles, a baby stroller used to tote tommy guns during getaways, and a matchbook from the Little Bohemia Lodge. There was no doubt about it. Dillinger was in Chicago.

In little more than a year, Dillinger had led six major bank robberies, killed two police officers, a civilian, and two FBI agents, escaped imprisonment twice, and eluded or shot his way out of a half-dozen cleverly-laid traps.

Prior to his death, the hardened gangster had been well aware of his streak of fortune and was none too secure about its future continuance. In May 1934, a skittish Dillinger had called his lawyer to discuss the prospect of plastic surgery. On the run from nearly every law enforcement agent in the country, the outlaw yet dared to hope for a new freedom, freedom which might be realized through the alteration of his well-known countenance and the obliteration of his infamous fingerprints. Accustomed to relying on none but himself and his gang for salvation, Dillinger was nonetheless prepared to put his money on one man, a surgeon by the name of Loeser. The gangster felt his trust was well placed, for he and his would-be doctor were birds of a feather: the latter had done time in Leavenworth on a narcotics charge. Sprung from his cage, Loeser was in dire need of funds. In payment for the surgeon's services, Dillinger opened his billfold to the tune of five grand.

Curtains for a Dirty Rat

On May 27th, the optimistic hood arrived on schedule for the promised procedure, met by his lawyer. In a derelict northside flat, owned by an ex-speakeasy operator, the two passed the night in expectation of the doctor's arrival the next day. When Loeser showed, however, the gangster and his counsel were disturbed to find him accompanied by a pallid and nerve-wracked young assistant. Soothed by the doctor's reassurances, the patient recited his wish list to the attentive Loeser: remove three moles and his giveaway scar; fill in his cleft chin and the bridge of his nose; and, most importantly, nix the damning fingerprints. Agreeing to the changes, Loeser showed Dillinger to a cot, instructed his assistant to administer a general anesthetic, and left the room to prepare for the operation. Placing an ether-soaked towel over Dillinger's nose and mouth, the assistant advised his charge to take some deep breaths. The patient obliged, with dire results. The flustered accomplice- had given the gangster a dangerous dosage and his face proceeded to turn blue. Then, to the young man's horror, Dillinger swallowed his tongue.

Summoned by his assistant's screams, Loeser grabbed his forceps and pulled Dillinger's tongue from his throat. The patient was not breathing. In a ramshackle flat on a quiet Chicago morning, the world's most wanted criminal was dead.

Thoroughly alarmed to action, Loeser worked furiously to restore respiration. After a few moments on the other side, Dillinger was revived, reassured, and re-anaesthetized. The surgery was resumed and completed to the gangster's satisfaction. Ironically, a mere 25 days later, Dillinger's new lease on life was bluntly terminated by a well-placed bullet from the frantic FBI.

At approximately 8:30 in the evening on July 22nd, the surgically-altered outlaw strolled into a screening of "Manhattan Melodrama" at the Biograph Theater on North Lincoln Avenue, observed by no less than 16 police officers and FBI agents, including Melvin Purvis himself. For two hours and four minutes, the watchers waited, one or another occasionally entering the theater to walk the aisles in search of their prey. When Dillinger finally emerged onto the sidewalk, his would-be captors were more than ready, but a little bit wary.

Public Enemy Number One he was, but he looked nothing like the romantic trench-coated antagonist noir that popular culture imagined. Instead, agents beheld a weary moviegoer on a hot summer night, clad in a straw hat, a gray-and-black flecked tie knotted onto a white silk shirt, canvas shoes, and gray summer trousers. Coatless, he appeared unarmed as well and must have undermined the resolve of more than a few of his stalkers, especially in light of his altered features. To Purvis, however, he was unmistakable: 'I knew him the minute I saw him. You couldn't miss if you had studied that face as much as I have.'

As the target strolled south on Lincoln Avenue, he stepped down a curb to a narrow alley entrance. As Dillinger turned down the passageway, a half dozen agents closed in. The moment froze as Dillinger, his back to the pack, instinctively went for a cleverly concealed .38–too late. Four shots were fired, three hitting their mark. Among a swarm of home-bound moviegoers and nearly a score of law enforcement officers, Dillinger went down. Chaos ensued.

According to the *Chicago Tribune,* Dillinger dropped at the feet of Mrs. Pearl Doss, a woman that recognized the fallen man as "Johnnie," a neighbor boy from her Indiana youth. Doss claimed that in that moment of recognition she was close enough to catch his classic last words: "They've got me at last."

A nearby barkeep mistook the victim for his brother-in-law, sending his wife into hysterics. Tradition tells of passers-by running to dip their handkerchiefs in the still-flowing blood, anxious for gruesome souvenirs of the startling event. Struggling for control, Purvis ordered that Dillinger be rushed to nearby Alexian Brothers Hospital. Dead on arrival, Dillinger's body was turned away at the doors. The strange party retired to the hospital lawn to await the deputy coroner.

Curtains for a Dirty Rat

That night the city awoke, electric. For weeks, Northsiders had been warned by police at the Town Hall and Sheffield district headquarters that the outlaw had been seen in Lakeview, North Center, and Uptown by various witnesses. A March 7th edition of the local Booster newspaper proclaimed:

> *LOOK UNDER YOUR BED. SEARCH YOUR CELLAR. SHAKE OUT THE MOTHBALLS FROM LAST SUMMER'S CLOTHES. DILLINGER IS HIDING SOMEWHERE HERE. AND HE MAY BE HIDING IN YOUR BACKYARD.*

One lifetime North Side resident, my aunt Frances Kathrein, recalled that sweltering July night in 1934, when she and her brothers and sisters lay sleeping on the front-room floor of their second-story flat, hoping for a breath of wind through the screen door. What wafted through that door was not a summer breeze, however, but a sudden sound of commotion on the street outside. Frances' future husband, Norbert, then 13 years old, tore down Cuyler Avenue with a group of newsboys full of papers and cries of "Extra!" and delivering in loud voices the news: "Dillinger's Shot!"

In a report shocking for its day, the *Chicago Tribune* reported on the mob scene at the Cook County morgue, where the line of curiosity-seekers snaked through the building, apparently oblivious to rows of exposed corpses, and stretched down the block outside. The coroner, a man by the name of Walsh, after viewing the crowd "with apparent satisfaction,"[40] posed for photographs with the body. At his instruction, Dillinger's corpse was placed in a basement room behind a glass panel so that the crowds might be allowed to file past for a look at the expired Enemy. The scene was as absurd as might be imagined, and the *Tribune* presented it in all its brutishness, focusing particular attention on the women in the crowd, who:

> *...pushed forward with massive shoulders and hips. Some of them sighed or groaned with a pretense of horror as they looked at the body, tilted at a 45- degree angle to give a*

---

[40] Chicago Tribune on Dillinger: viewed with apparent satisfaction

> better view. One or two with faces slightly less depraved than the others clucked their tongues and said as they went away: I wouldn't have wanted to see him except that I think it's a moral lesson, don't you? ... One fat blonde woman, after leaving the basement, applied fresh lipstick and, preparing to join the waiting line to have another look, said, 'I'm disappointed. Looks just like any other dead man.'[41]

The Biograph Theater manager declined a chance to speak to the press about the theater's role in the set-up, fearing possible ill-effects on his business. On the other hand, when one reporter, hoping to squeeze some information from Morris Oppenheimer, the proprietor of the bar next door, arrived at the tavern, he found that Oppenheimer had "already paint[ed] a sign, in blood-red letters, proclaiming:

DILLINGER HAD HIS LAST DRINK HERE

In light of the mania following Dillinger's death, it seems almost unbelievable that no unusual phenomena were reported at the shooting site in the immediate months and years that followed. In fact, it was not until the 1970s that passers-by on north Lincoln Avenue began to spot a bluish figure running down the alley, stumbling, falling, and disappearing. Accompanying such sightings were the typical reports of cold spots, feelings of uneasiness, and the sudden unwillingness to use the alley as a handy shortcut to Halsted Street.

In recent years, while paranormal tales of that alleyway have lapsed, its history and mystery remain. Visitors to the Biograph Theater can examine a diagram on the window of the old box office describing the complex set-up of Dillinger by Melvin Purvis' FBI. Led by the story, they can sit in the seat where Dillinger sat more than 60 years ago and afterwards emerge to walk his last path to the passage still known by older Chicagoans as "Dillinger's Alley." There, just beyond the pool of neon light shed by the

---

[41] Ibid.

Curtains for a Dirty Rat

theater's brilliant marquee, the imaginative and the perceptive might well wonder about the supernatural survival of that most reluctant of victims.

Dillinger's will to live may continue to inspire us to doubt his death, a doubt that echoes that of Mary Kinder, a friend of Dillinger's. Kinder had certainly read the news about the shoot-out in the alley and had talked with a legion of reporters the next morning about her reaction to the fugitive's demise. Despite the undeniable fact of Dillinger's demise, the girl couldn't help asking, as some still do, "Is it true? Is he dead?"

After the 1934 shootout in the Northwoods of Wisconsin, it wasn't only Dillinger's name that made world headlines. By the time the infamous shots rang out through the pines of Manitowish Waters, Dillinger was "Public Enemy Number One," but Lester Gillis, Dillinger's right-hand man, was surely Number Two.

It had been a long way to the top from juvenile delinquent to federal target. After stints in reformatories and jails as a boy and young man under his real name, Gillis resurfaced at the dawn of the '30s with a new name: George Nelson, aka "Baby Face," for his blue eyes and boyish looks.

In February of 1931, Nelson was arrested with several other men after a bank robbery and sentenced to Joliet Prison for a term of one year to life. A year later, he was taken from Joliet to stand trial in Wheaton for another bank robbing charge. He was found guilty again and sentenced to another year to life in Joliet Prison.

This was too much for Nelson. Arriving back at the Joliet depot with a prison guard, the pair got into a taxicab for the ride back to the prison, handcuffed together. As the cab neared Joliet prison, however, the guard felt the nose of a revolver against his cheek. Nelson leaned into the guard's ear and said, "Open the handcuffs."

The guard unlocked the cuffs, and Nelson took his gun. With a gun pointed at each man, Nelson ordered the driver to take him to a cemetery near the village of Summit, Illinois. There, he forced the cabbie and guard out of the car, took the wheel and sped away.

Law enforcement soon discovered Nelson's ties to Dillinger. Years of pursuit followed, with local and federal agents constantly on the move after the Indiana farm boy cum bank robber and his gang. A shootout at the Little Bohemia Lodge in Northwoods Mercer, Wisconsin in the spring of 1934 ended with Nelson shooting a federal agent dead. Dillinger and the gang escaped.

With the death of its kingpin, John Dillinger, in a Lincoln Avenue alleyway in Chicago that summer, the rest of the Dillinger gang was on the lam. The United States Division of Investigation (precursor to the FBI) was out to catch the rest of them—in particular the deadly and elusive Baby Face Nelson.

That fall, Nelson was holed up in his hideout in Lake Geneva, Wisconsin. Reports leaked through the grapevine that Nelson was planning a heist a day for a month, and federal agents were ready.

On November 27th, Nelson, his wife Helen, and another man, John Paul Chase, left for Chicago on U.S. Route 12 (current day Route 14).

When they neared the town of Fox River Grove, Illinois, Nelson recognized federal agents in an oncoming car. The agents, it turns out, recognized him too.

In a strange twist of events, Nelson ended up as the pursuer. Helen, driving the gang's car, bore down on the agents and the gangsters fired into the agents' car. The agents shot back and then turned off the highway. One of the agents' bullets had punctured the water pump on Nelson's car. They were quickly losing speed. A second federal car arrived on the scene, its two agents taking up the pursuit.

Curtains for a Dirty Rat

When he saw the new car gaining fast, Nelson told his wife to turn into Barrington's Northside Park. The agents' car at first passed by. Realizing they had overshot the turn, the agents stopped the car and got out, getting behind it with their weapons. Helen ran to hide, and Nelson and Chase took positions behind their own vehicle.

Next came what became known as the "Battle of Barrington": a vicious shootout between Nelson and Chase and the two federal agents.

One of the agents fired on Nelson with a submachine gun, a round hitting him in the liver and pancreas and exiting his back. After a bloody exchange, Special Agent Herman Hollis was struck with a bullet to the head, while Special Agent Samuel P. Cowley from a shower of fire from Nelson's tommy gun. Hollis was dead on arrival at a nearby hospital. Cowley soon after. The latter endured stomach surgery before dying of a stomach wound.

Nelson, badly wounded, transferred the gang's weapons into the agents' car and collapsed inside it. Chase took the wheel, speeding to a safe house in Wilmette. In the car, Nelson turned to Helen and said, "I'm done for."

At the house, Nelson was put into a bed. There, minutes later, Baby Face Nelson—John Dillinger's right hand man—died.

A phoned-in tip led police to Nelson's body, which had been wrapped in a Native American blanket and laid in front of St. Paul's Lutheran Cemetery in Skokie, Illinois.

Helen Gillis surrendered to federal agents after hiding in Chicago briefly. She went to prison for violating parole after her Little Bohemia arrest. Chase served time on Alcatraz Island.

Today, grandkids—now grandparents themselves—still tell of the night Baby Face Nelson escaped his return to Joliet Prison in 1931 to go on to become one of the most infamous of American criminals. When the cab never arrived at the prison, police believed Nelson might have killed his guard and the driver and escaped into the neighborhoods of Joliet. Residents locked their doors and slept with their guns, in case Nelson should come a-knocking, in search of shelter.

Little did anyone know, for several hours, that Nelson was far from Joliet.

These many years after the death of Baby Face Nelson in a North Shore safe house, Nelson's ghost continues to walk. He seems to be remorseful of his life of crime, for he favors the spots where his hand brought death, and not the site of his own.

For many years, visitors to the Little Bohemia Lodge in Mercer reported the sound of gunfire, which would awaken them at night in the cabins that used to be rented out there. Guests and the Lodge manager would search in vain for weapons on the property, and for the shooter. But despite the smell of gunpowder hanging in the air each time, nothing was ever found. They seemed to be auditory and olfactory apparitions.

In the northwest suburbs, visitors to North Barrington Park have from time to time reported the shadowy figure of a man, dressed in 1930s style clothing, walking through the park in the evening or standing near the park's memorial to the agents who lost their lives in the "Battle of Barrington."

THE WOOD WALKERS

On Chicago's Gold Coast, that exclusive lakefront enclave, ghosts are a dime a dozen, though not many are talked about by their ultra-chic flesh-and-blood housemates.

When, in 1885, Archbishop Patrick Feehan set up housekeeping in a lavish mansion on State Parkway, a large acreage surrounded the dwelling. For decades, the Chicago Gold Coast had kept its dead here, interred in the old

---

[42] Potter Palmer or a Gold Coast Mansion: Photo of Cardinal's Mansion (Archbishop's Mansion) via *Wikimedia Commons*
https://commons.wikimedia.org/wiki/File:Archbishops_House_Chicago.JPG

Ghosts of Lincoln Park

City Cemetery just beyond North Avenue. When the question of disease threw lakefront residents into a panic, the cemetery was closed and the bodies relocated to outlying sites along the Chicago and Northwestern rail line: Catholics went to Calvary, on the border between Chicago and Evanston, a town directly north of the city limits. The others were buried in Rosehill, bordered today by Ravenswood, Peterson, Western, and Berwyn Avenues.

With the corpses gone, the abandoned expanse was open for suggestions. Though any of a million developmental fates might have befallen it, a wonderful one awaited. In 1868, much of the land became Lincoln Park. The rest was sold off for residential development. Yet, while the lakefront and its adjacent neighborhood would become beautiful over the next half century, little did the earliest squatters know that this area was destined to become one of the swankiest neighborhoods in America. Little, too, did they realize that bodies from the empty cemetery would continue to turn up here for the next 100 years.

Fourteen years after the opening of Lincoln Park, Potter Palmer, Chicago's most influential businessman of the day, moved into a million-dollar castle at 1350 N. Lake Shore Drive, fleeing the elite community of Prairie Avenue, south of the city center. In a short time, Palmer's former neighbors followed suit, and the old burial ground began to really glimmer. From then on, Chicago's old and new money would consider the Gold Coast as the ultimate in city living.

Many of the sumptuous residences that arose from this former swamp still stand today, relics of an age of overkill. Living in them are a number of descendants of those first Chicago "haves" and a host of relatively new millionaires as well. Though their origins may vary, many have at least two things in common: they're loaded, and they're haunted.

Since the neighborhood's earliest days, Gold Coasters settling down on Dearborn Parkway, State Parkway, and Astor Street have been aware of a sort of shadow population living with them in these haunts of the rich and famous (a population hailing, presumably, from the old City Cemetery) and the remains that, despite the cemetery's relocation, remained right here, often under the foundations of their houses.

After the first run-ins with partially decomposed corpses during the groundbreaking of the early homes and the hasty disposal of the evidence, residents complained of strange goings-on in their dream homes. As these hauntings arose time and again, would-be builders listened well. Soon, an unspoken understanding prevailed among future homeowners: when remains were unearthed, no expense or effort was spared in properly burying the grisly find.

Even today, this silent pact holds true. When, just recently, at the end of the twentieth century, a wealthy businessman began the total renovation of a grand old structure on State Parkway, he was hardly surprised at the discovery of an early team of contractors and well prepared with an old neighborhood solution. One worker explains that when the renovation of the elegant brownstone began, the basement floor had to be opened up for plumbing, electrical, and ventilation work. The job had to be dug by hand, by pick and shovel, and the men digging the trenches unearthed human remains.

The general contractor on the job had a Native-American laborer, a very spiritual man. When the men working on the trench would disturb any remains, they were told to go upstairs and get this laborer, who would then come down and remove the remains to the side of the trench and say prayers over them.

A good background of the Gold Coast neighborhood is found in *Chicago: City of Neighborhoods*. The account of the accidental excavation on State Parkway was provided to the author in the summer of 2000 in a written account by an anonymous worker.

Ghosts of Lincoln Park

THE PRESIDENT, POST-MORTEM

[43] Lincoln's train: The funeral train enters Chicago under the massive arch built for the occasion. *Library of Congress*.

44

There can be no doubt that the ghost of President Abraham Lincoln is one of the most famed and prolific of all phantoms. It is the ghost of his *funeral*, however, that has intrigued so many Chicago fans of the late president after his assassination.

Each spring, trainspotters, Civil War buffs, presidential scholars and ghost hunters gather along the old route of Lincoln's funeral procession, which carried the president's embalmed body from Washington through seven major cities—including Chicago—finally arriving in Springfield, Illinois. They say that, if you are along the tracks in late April or early May, you may be one of the privileged few to see the ghost of the funeral train, complete with phantom Union soldiers standing guard, the filmy body of the president himself displayed in the hearse car, and even the throngs of

---

[44] Drawing of Lincoln's death in the bed, via *Library of Congress*

ghostly mourners flanking the tracks. Legend has it that, if you are lucky enough to view the ghost train, your watch will stop and never work again.

When the body of President Abraham Lincoln rolled into Chicago on its way to rest in Springfield, Illinois, the city was waiting. Passing through a 40-foot high arch that had cost more than $15,000 to build, the coffin was removed from its rail car and carried through a countless sea of mourners for display. This spare-no-expense attitude had been reflected as well in the lavish preparations of Baltimore, Harrisburg, Philadelphia, New York, Albany, Buffalo, Cleve-land, Columbus, and Indianapolis, each city striving to distinguish itself as the most gracious host of all.

Though the temporary surroundings varied, constant comfort was provided by the funeral car itself. Designed for Lincoln's use by the U.S. Military Railroad System, the car was run for the first time only after his death and was the grandest example of railcar construction of its time, complete with 16 wheels, expertly crafted woodwork, etched-glass windows, and upholstered walls. In addition, its wheels were cleverly designed to allow undisrupted travel across the irregularly-spaced rails that remained for years after Lincoln himself signed legislation standardizing the gauge between rails. The president would surely have been tickled.

Even cities not on the funeral route did their best to impress the now-unimpressible president: the mayor of St. Louis, for example, provided the $6,000 hearse, festooned with lavish plumes and striking trim, which awaited Lincoln in Springfield. And many towns along the route erected their own arches over the local railroad tracks in tribute. Perhaps most poignant was the one spanning the rails at Michigan City, Indiana, its epitaph gathering the sentiments of millions:

With Tears We Resign Thee to God and History

In Chicago, many believe the Chicago History Museum—the old Chicago Historical Society building in Lincoln Park—is also haunted by the ghost of Abraham Lincoln. The bed in which he died on Good Friday, 1865, is

Ghosts of Lincoln Park

permanently housed in the museum. They say that, sometimes at night, you can see the tall, dark figure of the dead president walking the halls of the institution. He pauses at the rear of the building, stopping for a minute at the windows overlooking the Lincoln Memorial in the park, before continuing his solitary night journey.

AUTHOR'S AFTERWORD

As twilight descends upon Chicago's Lincoln Park, the echoes of its storied past seem to become almost palpable. This beloved space is not merely a backdrop for soccer games, wedding photos and Sunday strolls; it is a repository of history marked by both triumph and tragedy. The ghosts of those who walked these grounds still linger, reminding us that while time moves forward, some stories refuse to fade.

As we've seen, Lincoln Park has witnessed significant events that shaped the city. The Great Fire of 1871 left an indelible mark on Chicago, transforming vast areas of the city and leading to the creation of this park as a place of solace amidst the chaos: a space shaped by the vision and potential of the 1893 World's Fair. Most have forgotten the horror that descended on the park on that terrible October night so long ago. But the ghosts seem to remember it well. Today, as you walk along its paths, you might reflect on the many souls who still rest—or roam—here, though their grave markings are now lost to time.

Lincoln Park has seen both the poorest and most frustrated of lives and the most triumphant, in the mansions of Astor Street and the tenements of Little Hell and Cabrini Green. But money can't buy respite from unhappy souls, as our stories have well told. In both the barest cinderblock and the poshest graystone, ghosts wander; ghosts speak.

As for the site of the lost High Bridge, once you know about this lost chapter of Chicago, the Lincoln Park lagoon is forever changed. Once you see into this part of the park's history, you can't unsee it, as they say. No longer an idyllic spot, there's a darkness that can never be shaken from the picturesque vista along Lake Shore Drive. Looking at the fishermen along its banks at dusk and dawn, you wonder, What have they seen? And What do they know?

Ghosts of Lincoln Park

As we've seen, the St. Valentine's Day Massacre of 1929, a violent chapter in Chicago's gangster lore, casts a long shadow. Though the events unfolded across the city, some of the strongest reverberations of the gangland era were felt in Lincoln Park, where the community struggled to make sense of the chaos and violence that marred not just their city, but their home streets . . . and a tiny garage on Clark Street on a bitterly cold morning.

As we close this exploration of Lincoln Park, we are left with an understanding that history is a living entity. Each monument, each tree, tells a story that connects us to those who came before. Each step passes above a literal final resting place of a man, woman or child who played a role in the drama of the "City of the Century." The spirits of this park invite us to remember, to reflect, and to acknowledge that while the events of the past may seem distant, they continue to shape our experiences today. This space, where the living coexist with the memories of the lost, offers a chance for connection—a reminder that we are part of a larger narrative.

The ghosts of Lincoln Park are not merely figments of imagination; they are reminders of the resilience of a city that has faced both triumph and tragedy. Let their stories guide you, urging you to engage with the world around you and to honor the memories that linger in this vibrant landscape.

ABOUT THE AUTHOR

Ursula Bielski is the founder of Chicago Hauntings and the host of WYCC PBS's The Hauntings of Chicago.

An historian, author, and parapsychology enthusiast, she has been writing and lecturing about Chicago's supernatural folklore and the paranormal for nearly twenty years and is recognized as a leading authority on Chicago and Midwest ghostlore and cemetery history. Her tours are the basis and foundation of our Chicagoland routes.

www.ingramcontent.com/pod-product-compliance
Lightning Source LLC
LaVergne TN
LVHW022325080426
835508LV00013BA/1315